To my sons . . .

DOWN TO CAMP:
A History of Summer Folk on Whidbey Island

by Frances L. Wood

Blue Heron Press
Mercer Island, WA 98040
USA

DOWN TO CAMP:
A History of Summer Folk on Whidbey Island

by Frances L. Wood

Published by: Blue Heron Press
                5200 Butterworth Road
                Mercer Island, WA 98040 USA
                (206) 232-4757

For individual orders send $13..95 (plus WA state sales tax of $1.14, if applicable) plus $3 for postage and handling to this address. Wholesale orders may also be submitted to this address.

No part of this book may be reproduced or transmitted in any form or by any means, electronic or mechanical, including photocopying, recording, or by any information storage-and-retrieval system, without written permission from the publisher. Brief passages may be quoted for reviews.

Cover and book design: Gery Rudolph
Proofing: Hanna Atkins

Copyright 1997 by Frances L. Wood
All rights reserved
First printing 1997
Printed in the United States of America

ISBN: 0-9656119-1-4

*This book was written for and is dedicated to
my sons, Munro and Alex. May going "down to camp"
forever remain firmly embedded in your bones.*

Acknowledgments

I wish to acknowledge and thank the many people who assisted with the completion of this work.

Bill Graves, my partner and husband, for careful editing and loving support; Joan and Chuck Bakeman, for historical research, encouragement, family stories, and manuscript review; Harriet Fulton Putnam, for family stories and remembrances.

Also, I wish to thank: Susan Ross, Ana Kinkaid, my Goal Group (individually and collectively), The South Whidbey Historical Society, The Snohomish Historical Museum, and The Whidbey Institute.

All photos from the Wood family collections, except those from: Chuck and Joan Bakeman, page 11, 67; Harriet Fulton Putnam, pages 52, 58, 69; Janet Sue Carpenter Terry, pages 26, 44; The South Whidbey Historical Society, pages 55, 57; The Whidbey Institute, pages 30, 56.

Contents

DOWN TO CAMP:
A History of Summer Folk on Whidbey Island

Chapter 1	DOWN TO CAMP	7
Chapter 2	EARLY CLINTON HISTORY	21
Chapter 3	A CAMP TO FISH AND DIG CLAMS	33
Chapter 4	A 150-FOOT WATERFRONT LOT	43
Chapter 5	CAMP ILLAHEE	61
Chapter 6	BEACH FICTION	75
Chapter 7	DRIFT INN	83
Chapter 8	PRESENT GENERATION	95
Chapter 9	CONCLUSION	103
	Footnotes	107
	Family Tree	113
	History of Cabin Ownership	115

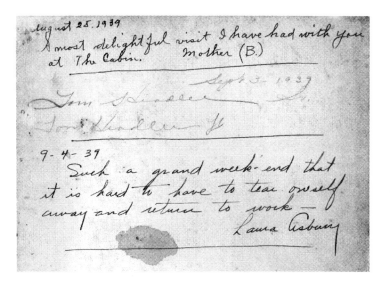

First page of cabin log, 1939. At the end of each visit to the cabin we write in the log.

Chapter 1

DOWN TO CAMP

The first entry in the cabin log was dated August 25, 1939. It reads:

> "A most delightful visit I have had with you at the Cabin. Mother (B.)" —*Nina Blackman Bakeman*

For five generations our family has been going "down to camp" at a funky walk-in beach cabin on Brighton Beach at Clinton, Whidbey Island, Washington. For close to one hundred years, the Blackman, Bakeman, Fulton, Wood, Carpenter, and now Galloway, Oyler, and Graves clans have fished, clammed, picnicked, beachcombed, boated, and relaxed on the same shore with one of Puget Sound's most spectacular views. We have escaped our city life, retreated, written books, vacationed, and celebrated. Throughout the generations, no one ever moved permanently to the Island; we have always remained summer folk. But year after year, generation after generation, like migrating birds, we return. When the spring rains take a break and the weather starts to warm, talk turns to a weekend at the cabin. And another season begins.

Our camp, Drift Inn, in 1958. My father, Amos, collected barrels for seating and painted names on them. Side porches were for open-air sleeping, girls on the left and boys on the right.

It is very apropos that the first entry in our cabin log is from Mother B. She, I believe, is our original link to this shore. The story, however, begins decades prior to the 1939 entry, perhaps as early as 1887. Mother B, a spry, tiny package of energy called Nina Blackman, had just moved to Washington Territory to begin teaching school in Snohomish.

The history of the Blackman family settling in Snohomish is well documented. The Snohomish Historical Museum is housed in the former home of Nina's cousin, Hyrcanus Blackman. Also, the history of the permanent settlement of South Whidbey and the village of Clinton has been researched and published in a two-volume set entitled, *South Whidbey and Its People*.

This is the previously untold story of the summer folk on one specific beach on South Whidbey. It is, however, a beach story that is told again and again in differing formats on beaches up and down Puget Sound. It is the story of escape from city life, the story of finding renewal in a spectacularly beautiful environment. It is the story of searching for the richness and creativity at the core of our being.

It is also the story of why. Why are we drawn like homing pigeons to this one speck of land when we now have the choice to travel almost anywhere in the world? Why are we still attracted to the simple natural feeling of the beach? Why does it feel deep in our bones that we are going home, finding our roots, when we visit the beach? Why do we spend hours walking the beach looking for agates or just sitting on the beach gazing out over the water and sifting the warm dry sand gently through our mindless fingers?

Our family goes to a beach cabin but "down to camp" is really a state of mind and can happen in many venues. Your "camp" may be a farm retreat. It may be a favorite moss-covered rock next to a softly cascading stream. It may be a mountain top. A boat with a cabin for sleeping, even a favorite bed and breakfast inn can supply the sanctuary for your body and soul to escape to a simple, creative respite of refreshment and healing.

All these sanctuary retreats may provide the same thing as our cabin. They allow us to slow down and escape our all-too-busy city-life agenda. The retreats provide the refreshment of creativity, which has become absent from many of our lives. They encourage us to experience nature first hand. A feeling of exploration and adventure is possible. They give us an excuse to simplify our lives.

In 1976 four generations of my family were gathered in a scattering of vintage rocking chairs on the front porch of the circa 1915 two-story cedar beach house. Eyes gazed across Possession Sound, a fat arm of Puget Sound, to Hat Island and the mainland with Everett at the shoreline and the snow-peaked Cascade Mountains at skyline. The porch roof protected the family grouping from the glaring midday sun and the light north breeze turned the ever-changing bay into a deep blue. Gulls called across the tide flats ripening with the fragrance of seaweed and salt. On the sandy beach, two bathing suit-clad boys and a black lab were industriously building today's sand castle, a race with the tide that they never won.

"Why do you call it 'down to camp'?"

"Why do you call it 'down to camp'?" he questioned. I looked at the quizzical expression on the tan face of my young son and saw that serious, I-need-a-real-answer look. So I repeated his question to the assembled family.

"Seriously, why does everyone in our family call it 'down to camp' when it is obvious that we go north (up rather than down) to stay at the family beach cabin on Whidbey Island?"

Great-grandmother, Inez, (also known as Honey) broke the stillness. "Well, now that doesn't make sense anymore, does it?" She continued, "When I was a girl we would pack our things in a boat in Snohomish where we lived, and go down the Snohomish River. The River empties into Possession Sound right across the bay there at Everett. Can you see where I'm pointing? We came across to this very beach and camped. Thus, 'down to camp.' After a while we built tent platforms and cabins. Several families from Snohomish joined us." I could almost hear the pieces of understanding silently falling together in my son's mind. The statement also explained why the inhabitants of many of the 30 or so cabins on the beach seemed related. Close friends back in 1900, the families were well intertwined by now.

Eating watermelon on the bulkhead in 1938.

Left to right, back row: Nina Bakeman Blackman, Frances Bakeman Hodge, Donna MacKenzie Bakeman, Paul William Hodge, Charles (Dick) Bakeman, Paul H. Hodge. Front row: Jim Bakeman, Chuck Bakeman, and John Hodge.

The flavor of going "down to camp" has always been influenced by its setting. Several environmental factors have helped preserve a camp-like atmosphere. The cabins, strung out along the beach, are backed by a high, unscaleable bluff that leaves no room for a road. Since originally all the visitors arrived by boat, no road was necessary. That worked fine until, a generation later, a ferry connected the Island to the mainland south of Everett. Then everyone began arriving by car down Brighton Beach Road. The welcoming community built a footpath in front of each cabin, allowing summer folk living away from the road-end to walk to their cabins. Since the early 1930s, the family parked the car at the road-end to the south and walked along an elevated boardwalk, and then down a pathway in front of 19 cabins to ours. One consequently begins to think twice about what one wants to carry "down to camp." The walk in to our cabin also provides the perfect excuse to retain the simple cabin feeling and leave our city toys in the city. During the following generation, Hastings Road was built at the north end of the beach, and now the walk to our cabin is only a nine-cabin walk from that road-end.

There is another influence of the bluff that tends to keeps the cabins simple and rustic. Occasionally it decides to slide. Generally every winter there is some slipping and sliding into back yards causing a mess, but no real damage. During my grandmother Inez's early adult years, the bluff let loose mud, brush, and trees with such force that a tree trunk went slamming into her sister Frances's cabin two to the north. That tree crashed in the back door and came out the front door. Around 1930 the sliding bank totally destroyed the small guest cottage located to the north of our main cabin. A dormant period followed.

Inez Bakeman Fulton with daughter Elaine in 1915. Notice the sandy beach with beach logs. Now a seven-foot bulkhead separates the cabin property from the incoming tide.

Recently the cliff awakened again, and with vengeance picked up Aunt Frances's old house (two to the north) and deposited it in the bay. The worst was cleared back from the pathway and now we walk over a mound of compacted mud and brush on our way to our cabin. It is a hard push with a wheelbarrow full of groceries, bags, fishing poles, and gas for the lawn mower.

The bluff changes and also the beach changes. The old picture of my grandmother in her white lacy dress sitting on a log with her first-born daughter, Elaine (my mother), on her lap, shows a sandy beach with logs. Over the years the beach has lowered and there is a now a seven-foot high bulkhead holding the high tide back from the lawn in front of the cabins.

The potholes are another example of change. My father, Amos, came from Ohio. When he moved west as a young engineer to work for Boeing, he quickly made up for his upbringing deprived of an ocean. Dad liked to fish. Actually he liked to be out on the water slowly putt-putting down the bay with no demands or responsibilities; fishing was the excuse. He listened to the old salts on the beach to find out the best fishing spots. Fifty feet or so off the old Shell Dock was one favorite spot. That was easy, remnants of the old Shell Dock still stood about a half-mile to the south at Randall Point. Also, the fishing was good opposite the old Brickyard. Concrete monolithic artifacts identify that spot. But the potholes, the best fishing spot, were elusive. They were supposedly somewhere off Hastings Road where the normally long shallow tide flats were indented with two deep holes, perfect for fish to hang out, thinking they were safe. I was nearing the age of 40 before I realized the potholes simply weren't there anymore. Walking the beach at low, low tide revealed no indentations in the beach geography. The superficially static beach had changed, the pot holes were filled and the sand in front of the cabins, perhaps a quarter- to a half-mile away, was gone.

Last year National Geographic published a map supplement with all the known faults around the globe, and when I zeroed in on Puget Sound, there, crossing the south end of Whidbey Island, is the South Whidbey Fault. We know that mud slides and moving sand are distinctly different from earthquakes, but somehow knowing that our beach is located on a named fault makes all the change understandable.

If I hadn't spent vacations at the beach cabin, I would have grown up thinking that the land and seashore stay the same and that people change. But I know the opposite is true: the earth moves, but people stay the same. Looking at the old photo of my grandmother, I too can hear the lullaby of sounds as the waves whisper against the beach on a calm afternoon. I can feel the wispy locks of hair tickling my nose from a child sitting on my lap. I sense that pure light feeling of a timeless beach afternoon. These and a million more bits and pieces are the never-changing reality of going "down to camp."

We three owners, my brother Dick, sister Nancy, and myself, consciously keep the cabin, named Drift Inn, simple and eclectic. Simple means there is no TV or video. Radios are stored in our personal closets. There is no clock except for the tide clock, which tells how many hours before or after low or high tide. Dishes are washed by hand. Laundry is taken into town. The 1960s brought indoor plumbing and the 1980s hot water. Finally, last year we installed a phone line for emergencies or for our convenience. Dick was firmly against this intrusion to our peace and privacy, so Nancy and I had to sneak this one past him. We don't leave the phone set plugged in, hide it in a closet, and he hasn't noticed the change.

The cabin holds four generations of personal attachment. A watercolor painting of Mt. Rainier—naive and simple, by my mother's cousin Paul William Hodge, who became a noted astronomer but never a renowned artist—hangs in the stairs up to the second floor loft. I watched him paint it and remember how he used a toothbrush to scatter drops of brightly colored paint to suggest wild flowers in a meadow. The beach somehow encourages this kind of playful creativity. An astronomer can be an artist for the day, and the cabin proudly displays the results.

Examining sealife in about 1920. Hat Island is in the background.

Left to right: Reed Fulton in hat with hands on hips, four busy women, and male friend playing with starfish.

A needlepoint of a bouquet of flowers made by my mother, a ship's lantern from an unknown ship, a decoy forgotten by the first owners, has each found a permanent home at the cabin. Sleeping bags from my brother's first wife bedeck bunk beds from my brother's second wife, which all jumble together, accepting anyone needing a place to sleep. Plastic dishes that just won't break mix with chipped china cups and square melmac plates. Choosing a bowl for cereal can become a dilemma, do I use Aunt Frances's china, practical grandma Inez's plastic, or former sister-in-law Lee's ceramic? The memories of past generations are fused into the cabin like barnacles on an aging piling.

Remember the old Shell Dock where the fishing was good? That dock was used in my grandmother's early years for the steamer from the mainland to drop off people and supplies for the community. Now the few remaining pilings provide seating for gulls and cormorants. The old Brickyard to the north produced sandlime bricks that were too soft and sandy for the business to be a lasting success. I remember being able to see through the back of the fireplace shortly before we dismantled it. Yet, a few residual gray bricks remain as a hearth supporting our wood-burning stove.

Fish print by Dick Wood. This and other craft projects decorate our beach cabin.

One other former business on the beach is the Sawdust Dock where an auger was used to carry sawdust from a mill on top of the bluff out to barges. Its skeleton remains about a mile to the north, beyond the cabins, where the beach is uninhabited. Somehow, at the cabin, it feels good to be in a place where businesses are gone but their relics remain as visible reminders of the past.

"Down to camp" is much more than a physical place, it is a state of mind. One saying my mother often repeated, having heard it from her mother and her grandmother before her, was, "You can do what you want at camp." A simple phrase with profound meaning. I can imagine the relief of the original Blackman ancestors leaving the strict mores of the Victorian life in Snohomish and finding the freedom to be natural and carefree at the beach. Today we abandon the demands of our much-too-busy lives as we cross on the ferry and relax into the soothing opiate of the beach.

If our cabin ever falls into line and becomes the next one to land in the bay, (touch wood) and I could save only one thing, it would be the cabin log. Since the first entry by my great-grandmother, Mother B, there have been some gaps, but for the last two generations we have regularly recorded our visits and activities. Sizes of fish and who caught them are always noted, as are the number of crabs the crab pot attracted, and what bait was used. Visitors are requested to write a comment, a nice one. Special events are memorialized. My brother, dressed in a tux jacket, shorts, and going barefooted, was married at the cabin. My husband and I decided to get married while digesting the most delicious spicy clam fettuccine. All of this is in the log, as are bird species seen, what the weather was like, what projects need doing, and how my sister's dog Otis related to the other beach dogs.

The fishing gets better for a time and then it drops off. Orca whale pods are spotted about once a year, and about once in ten years a stray gray whale wanders into our corner of Puget Sound. Eagle families roost in an old snag up on the bluff directly above our cabin and nest just south of Randall Point. Barn swallows chatter persistently and then swoop by our ears as they try each spring to nest right over the front door. At the cabin it's hard to avoid getting close to nature.

Actually, nobody calls it "down to camp" any more. But we do all the same things. I pick wildflowers for a bouquet on the table. Without TV or video we play gin rummy or even Old Maid if the deck of cards isn't complete. We do a lot of gazing out over the ever-changing water. We slow down. We read. We watch the tide come in and go out again. We find the rhythm of the beach, and we slow down enough to match it.

Reading back through the cabin log I am reminded again how generation after generation we remain the same. The log entries in the 1940s and 1950s could be made today. In the spring we write about the slides of the winter, how the sand is washing out or building up in front of the bulkhead, and how the grass has grown three feet high. In the summer we have big clam feeds, shirttail relatives drop in, the septic tank backs up. We carry coffee cans with string handles around our necks as we hike to the road and up the bluff to pick delicious wild blackberries for pie.

In the fall we gather fire wood off the beach, and watch the fall bird migrants. I bundle up and take one last aimless beach walk. I soak in all I can of the calling gulls, foam-fringed waves, and let the cool breeze cleanse me one more time. I breathe deeply, hoping to absorb enough of the beach to last until spring. Someone in the family, usually my brother, takes a day-trip to the cabin around Thanksgiving to close it down for the winter. He drains the water system, wraps the pipes, and shuts off the water. The season ends.

Cabin log sample page from 1977. Over the years the log has provided a living history of going "down to camp."

"Who were the first people to discover this beach?" asked my always inquisitive and bright-eyed five-year-old.

Inez's soft blue eyes first smiled at her great-grandson then rested on the wide expanse of the bay. "Well, the Indians, I guess. The story of our connection to the beach really starts with Nina and Charles. Nina Blackman Bakeman was my mother..."

DOWN TO CAMP: A History of Summer Folk on Whidbey Island

I notice my young son's interest waning and the progress on the sand castle pulling him toward the beach. As he scampers away, I promise to write it all down for him to remember. And finally, twenty years later, here it is.

Sand castle with moat in 1979. My sons Alex Galloway at left, amd Munro Galloway at right, with bulkhead behind.

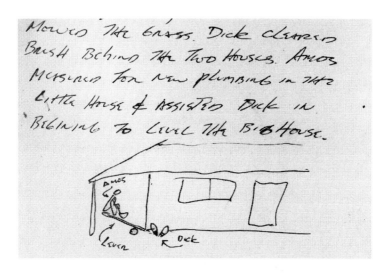

Cabin log entry, June 12, 1971. An old cabin always provides maintenance projects. Here Amos shows how he and Dick leveled the sagging southeast corner.

Chapter 2

EARLY CLINTON HISTORY

Sitting on the porch we gaze upon an almost 180-degree view of water. North toward Sandy Point on Whidbey Island then northeast to the south tip of Camano Island, farther east past Hat Island (referred to as Gedney Island on some maps) to Everett, south to Mukilteo and around to Randall Point on Whidbey again. We are not the first to regard this area as one entity. Our sweeping expanse encompasses almost the entirety of Possession Sound. This Sound crossed and fished by the Snohomish tribe for uncounted generations was first visited by Europeans in 1791. Captain George Vancouver landed near what later became Everett and officially took *possession* of the area in the name of King George III. The waters of our view thus became Possession Sound.

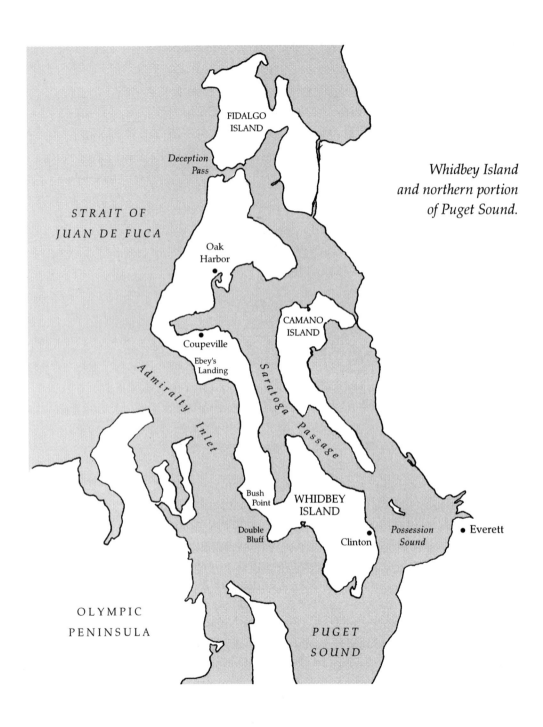

Whidbey Island and northern portion of Puget Sound.

Captain George Vancouver directed Master Joseph Whidbey to explore the eastern channels and shores of Puget Sound. His explorations revealed the narrow passage at the extreme north end of Whidbey Island, now called Deception Pass, and determined this land mass to be, in fact, an island. Vancouver rewarded Whidbey by naming after him the second longest island in what would become the lower forty-eight states, second only to Long Island in New York State. This skinny, lumpy island, 60 miles long and an average of eight miles wide, starts in Puget Sound, snakes north past Admiralty Inlet and the Strait of Juan de Fuca, and finally ends with its head nestled into Fidalgo Island, east of the San Juan Islands.

Whidbey Island receives less rainfall than the state of Kansas or Nebraska—a yearly average of 22.5"—thanks to its location in the rain shadow of the mountains of the Olympic Peninsula to the southwest. The mild average temperature of 50 degrees and abundance of fish and sea bounty provided a relatively easy existence first to the Native Americans, then the early white settlers, and now the summer folk.

Allan's Island near Deception Pass in 1886. Small steamers or launches deposited passengers on the beach to picnic or camp, similar to how our relatives arrived on Clinton Beach.

DOWN TO CAMP: A History of Summer Folk on Whidbey Island

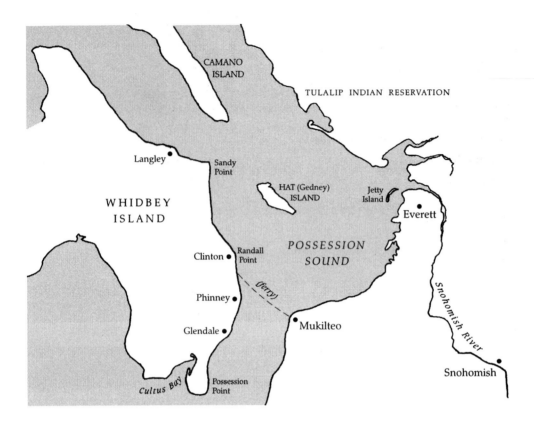

Possession Sound with Whidbey, Hat (Gedney), and Camano Islands. The Snohomish River empties into the Sound from lower right.

Twenty years after Vancouver, in 1811, with the founding of Fort Astoria at the mouth of the Columbia River, explorers and settlers gradually moved into the area of what was later to become western Washington. Marcus Whitman established his mission in Walla Walla in 1836 assisting overland visitors to this area. In 1841, Captain Wilkes visited the northern part of Whidbey, and by 1845 a settlement was established in south Puget Sound in the Tumwater area.

The natural prairies of northern Whidbey attracted settlement prior to the heavily forested areas of south Whidbey. The first attempt at settlement by a non-native on Whidbey Island was by Thomas W. Glasbow in 1848. He attempted to settle on the northern prairies around Ebey's Landing but the Indians of this region protested and the settlers left the land. Two years later Col. I. N. Ebey ignored the warning and consequently was killed by the Indians in 1857. But the tide was turning and settlers were appearing on various shores.

The Indians who greeted the first settlers on South Whidbey belonged to a different tribe of natives, the Snohomish. They looked upon Possession Sound as one unit with villages on the shores encircling the Sound. There were three Snohomish settlements on Whidbey and one on Camano Head with the Snohomish tribal headquarters located across the bay near Tulalip, north of Everett.

The largest Snohomish settlement was situated at Cultus Bay near the southern tip of Whidbey, where a large ceremonial potlatch house and six or seven longhouses provided for a village of 60-70 families. This village called Digwadsh was an important potlatch center for Indians traveling up and down the Sound. Two additional Snohomish villages on South Whidbey were established at what are now called Sandy Point and Bush Point. Each of these villages also included a potlatch house. (When Master Whidbey sailed past the Snohomish settlement at Sandy Point in 1791, he noted in his journal of seeing about 200 inhabitants.) During the summer and fall months the natives established temporary camps where they hunted, fished, and gathered clams and other sea life, which they dried and preserved for the winter.

The first non-Indian settler on South Whidbey was a 26-year-old man from Virginia named Robert Bailey. The friendly Snohomish and abundance of nature's bounty attracted him to the Digwadsh settlement on the southern tip of the Island in 1850. Two years later, he married a woman from the village and filed a claim on the land around Bailey's Bay, now called Cultus Bay. Here he established a trading post and set up a successful trading business with four Indian nations. William Jewett settled next to Bailey and became his son-in-law.

Sandy Point beach community in 1922. This area was originally called Brown's Point.

In 1859, a 19-year-old Portuguese seaman, Joseph Brown, jumped ship and landed in the Indian village at Sandy Point. Perhaps he was hiding from something, we do not know, but we do know he won the friendship of the natives there and settled into their life. He soon built a primitive lighthouse on the beach to define the point for steamers rounding that point on their way up and down Saratoga Passage. (I remember as a child playing on the old wooden hulk of a shipwreck resting on the beach just south of Sandy Point, which proves the need for the service Brown provided with his lighthouse.) The ship captains recognized this service by calling the village Brown's Point. After five years Brown married a 14-year-old Indian girl later called Mary. He built a large house up on the bluff above the beach to house his expanding family of 14 children.

The name Brown's Point lasted until 1916 when the area was purchased by several Everett men, who changed the name to

Sandy Point to attract buyers to their summer colony development. The name change must have paid off, as Sandy Point became a popular spot for summer folk, much more up-scale than our beach.

Settlers continued to arrive on south Whidbey and began to notice the area around Clinton. The original Clinton settlement was located north of the present ferry dock in the area of the old Shell Dock. Here the shoreline makes a rounded point called Randall Point, after Rosebury Randall, who acquired property here in 1913. Remains of the old Shell Dock can be seen about one-half mile south of our cabin. The area of the original settlement is now referred to as Old Clinton or Clinton Beach, since the present-day Clinton has spread to include the commercial area up on the hill, along highway 525. Although settlers had been homesteading on South Whidbey since the 1850s, Clinton became the first real town, starting in about 1875.

The origins of Old Clinton are intertwined with the origins of a settlement called Phinney located about two miles south of the ferry dock. During the 1850s and 1860s the thick stands of timber of south Whidbey were eyed by individuals and companies. A lucrative market for the timber was the booming town of San Francisco, swelling with the effects of the gold rush. The cedar tree was especially valuable for wharves, given its ability to withstand deterioration from the elements. In 1864 a California firm, Amos, Phinney, and Company, started purchasing large tracts of land along the eastern shores of Whidbey Island from north of what is now Langley south to near Glendale. The owners of the firm, Zachariah Amos, Arthur Phinney, and William H. Hooke, also retained part interest in a Port Ludlow lumber mill. It is assumed that much of the downed timber was shipped to Port Ludlow for milling. Once milled into

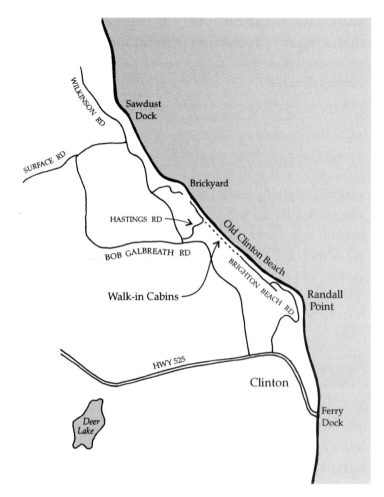

Map of Clinton Beach.

lumber, it was transported to San Francisco, the headquarters of the firm, to be used in construction in that city.

Arthur Phinney purchased the land around Glendale from his company. In 1877 he died and the piece of land, after a long and complicated process, came into the possession of Arthur's brother, John G. Phinney. John at the time was living in Port Ludlow, but moved to the South Whidbey land and began a settlement bearing his name. He also started a post office and began dealing in real estate. He sold the 120 acres that later became the town of Langley. John Phinney tired of running the post office in Phinney and moved it to the growing new settlement at Clinton in 1885. For seven years the post office was known as Phinney-Clinton, until 1892, when it officially became just Clinton.

The specific area of Old Clinton, the settlement along the beach at Randall Point, began to see the first meager attempts of settlement soon after 1872. Edward Hinman, a native of Clinton County, Michigan, headed west and began looking for a place to settle. Hinman, who had just finished service in the Civil War, joined a wagon train headed for San Francisco. Once there he heard stories of opportunities up north in Washington Territory. He secured passage on a sailing ship and disembarked once he reached the Puget Sound area. Hinman spent considerable time looking over the area and decided on the spot that became his home.

> "The site he selected, on the beach on the eastern shore about midway between Brown's Point and the village of Phinney, was an excellent choice for many reasons but especially because a fresh water creek ran down the hill above the settlement and provided water for all the steamers plying the Sound between Whatcom (Bellingham) and Olympia. The steamers were wood-burners so cord wood as well as water was needed."[1]

Shortly after Hinman built the dock at the village of Clinton, it became one of the busiest wharves in northern Puget Sound. Woodcutters were attracted to the area and soon a mill was built. In 1884 Hinman opened a store at the wharf at Clinton.

Merchandise was shipped from Seattle for the store and the steamer holds were refilled with cordwood and cedar shingles from the mill. Jacob Anthes, who later founded the town of Langley, owned 120 acres of timber in the area of old Clinton and supplied 35 cords of wood per day for the steamers.

The Ark owned and operated by Dallas Salisbury. The launch was used to carry party-goers to the docks along the beaches of South Whidbey.

Following the completion in 1894 of the Great Northern Railway into Bellingham, the need for steamers plying up and down Puget Sound dramatically decreased. Launches were used to service the few settlers on Whidbey. As the population of the Island increased around the turn of the century, the steamers were activated once again to service the Island.

Prior to 1900 there were no roads to speak of on South Whidbey. People and goods traveled by boat, and the wharf became the umbilical cord to the outside world. The early merchant boats on the Sound, called trade boats, acted as mobile stores for the villages sprouting up on South Whidbey. Often boats specialized in certain goods. As the name implies, merchandise could be purchased not only with coin, which was quite scarce, but also with trade goods, which the captain would add to his store and barter farther along his route. One popular local commodity was dogfish oil, which was collected by the trade boats and sold by the barrel to sawmills and logging camps. Hand-split shakes leaving the Clinton dock were sold for $2.00 per thousand. Other traded items were dried fish, wild duck feathers, hides and fur pelts.[2]

The glowing report of this beautiful benign climate and bountiful opportunity reached Edward Hinman's brother Henry who resided back in Michigan. Henry Hinman followed his brother west in 1884 and bought much of the land on the hill above the beach settlement of Clinton and north along the bluff. Henry lived for a time at Brown's Point and then built a house on the bluff near what is now called Wrightsman Place off Bob Galbreath Road.

By 1886 Edward Hinman, ready for a new adventure, turned the store and post office over to his brother Henry, and headed north to seek his fortune in the Alaskan gold fields. Reports returned to Clinton that Edward did find his fortune, but neither he nor his bounty made it back to Puget Sound. On the trip back he died, perhaps the result of foul play, and was buried at sea. No fortune accompanied the few belongings returned to his brother, Henry.

The less adventurous Henry Hinman remained in the Clinton area and lived to a respectable age. During his life Henry watched a great deal of change to our beloved beach. From his house on the bluff he observed our ancestors arrive by launch to camp on his beach. When they showed an interest in purchasing land, he was willing to sell. Our present lot was purchased from him on-the-spot on a sunny August day in 1902.

In 1910 a description of Henry Hinman shows his versatility and ambition.

> "Mr. H. C. Hinman owns a farm and orchard of 100 acres near Clinton, where he raises the usual farm crops. Mr. Hinman also operates the Hotel at Clinton, and has been instrumental in locating many summer resident there."[3]

Henry Hinman must also have been a patient man, since our ancestors camped on his property prior to purchasing it rather than patronizing his hotel.

Cabin log entry, 1975. Our "camp" has been a refuge for almost 100 years.

Chapter 3

A CAMP TO FISH AND DIG CLAMS

"The first Old Clinton Beach people all were originally from the State of Maine. The State of Mainers built Snohomish, the four Blackman brothers leading the way. In the early 1890s there was a boat called the *Wili-Wili* in which the Snohomish people would come down the Snohomish River over to Columbia Beach and camp out in tents and tent-cabins. They weren't interested in building houses or even buying property at that time, but would come to fish and dig clams."[1] —*George Clark IV*

The fondness for salt water beaches, fishing, and shellfish must have been deep and strong in the souls of our State of Maine ancestors when they arrived to help settle the town of Snohomish, Washington Territory. The town of Snohomish, positioned 12 miles upstream from Puget Sound, could not satisfy their marine longing. However, the warm sandy beaches down river and directly across Possession Sound not only satisfied that longing, but also indulged them in a summer "camp." A place to play and relax.

Standing on low sandy Jetty Island at the mouth of the Snohomish River with a present-day pair of high-powered binoculars, one can clearly see a row of summer cabins tucked under the cliff on the far shore, across seven miles of semi-protected Possession Sound. Our early ancestors, the Blackman brothers, could direct their launch in a straight line from the mouth of the River to our beach, with a stop, if desired, halfway across at the southern tip of Hat Island.

The town of Snohomish, positioned twelve miles upstream from Puget Sound, could not satisfy their marine longing.

Who were these people who came to fish and dig clams? The Blackman brothers were descended from a long line of Maine Yankees. During the 1600s these forebears left England, leaving behind that restrictive heritage, and after settling in this new continent became proud New Englanders. By 1872, several members of the extended Blackman family were ready to move west and look for fortune along the Pacific Ocean border of our developing United States.

When my great-grandmother Nina Blackman (Mother B) reached the age of nine, her parents, George and Frances (Eddy) Blackman, left Bangor, Maine, and moved their family first to Saginaw, Michigan, and then on to Oakland, California. George accepted a position as the California agent for the National Cash Register Company with his office in the San Francisco area. The family made their home in Oakland in 1876 where Nina and her brother Arthur were raised and educated.

While George headed for Oakland and the more refined life in business, three of his cousins, Alanson, Elhanon, and Hyrcanus Blackman made their way, in the fall of 1872, from Bradley, Maine, to the area around Snohomish.* These Blackman brothers, as they became known, were the sons of Adam and Mary Howard Blackman. A fourth Blackman brother, William, moved to the Seattle area, and an older sister, Mary Blackman Lenfest, later joined her brothers in Snohomish. After arriving in Snohomish, the three Blackman brothers cut timber and established several large mills. All three names were listed on the letterhead along with this description of the business: "Blackman Bro's, Lumber Manufacturers and dealers in General Merchandise. Sole proprietors of Blackmans' Patent Logging Car and Locomotive." Elhanon invented the tripper shingle machine, and Alanson was the inventor and patent holder of the Blackman logging truck.

The Blackman brothers also were instrumental in founding the town of Snohomish. Hyrcanus was the first mayor, elected in 1890 when the town was incorporated with a population of 2,012. He also served in the State Legislature and on the Snohomish School Board.

Ten years after the Blackman brothers arrived in Snohomish, another family with a similar sounding name but a very different background, the Bakemans, ventured west and found their way to Snohomish. The family's second son, Charles, was entrusted with the family savings of $1,800 and sent west to find a new family home. After stops in both Portland, Oregon, and Seattle, Washington Territory, he settled on Snohomish, then a village of 300 people. Word was sent back to Pestigo, Wisconsin, for Charles's parents and siblings to follow him west.

* See FAMILY TREE on pages 112-113.

Charles Henry Bakeman, my great-grandfather, in 1890. He was later called Dick.

Shortly after arriving in Snohomish, Charles started the first of his many business ventures, a furniture-building shop. In an article in the Seattle Post Intelligencer written in 1949, Charles described this early business venture, "Down at the mill I found some nice supplies of dry, clean alder and maple for $12 a thousand. I built a bench and the first thing I made was a chest of drawers." The popular item that first year turned out to be box springs. Every family in town wanted box springs. "I was making money. For six weeks all I made was box springs." His furniture business grew, and later employed several men and supplied furniture to the pioneers of the community. He branched out to a home-furnishing store.

Nina Blackman Bakeman, my great-grandmother, in her wedding dress, June 20, 1887.

Charles is credited with making the first buggy ever built in Snohomish County in 1883 and—an even greater accomplishment since there were no roads in the area—he sold the buggy! After a request to construct a wooden casket, Charles gradually worked his way into running a mortuary as well as the furniture store. Later he became the county coroner.

The story of Nina Blackman and Charles Bakeman is a wonderful love story that deserves a volume of its own. Theirs is a story of two lives coming together from very different backgrounds and social positions.

Charles was rugged, rough around the edges, from a solid German stock, recently emigrated. He was full of passion and ingenuity. Frances Bakeman Hodge described her father Charles thus, "My father's tales were peppered with words from the Chinook jargon. He often spoke of his friends as 'tillikums' and Indians as 'siwashes.' 'Skookum' meant strong and vigorous. 'Cultus' was the word for lazy. When we children were 'cultus,' mother applied the kindling stick."[2]

Nina, on the other hand, was the product of a genteel New England heritage whose family had been on this continent since the 1620s. Charles liked to play cards; she did not. He liked to dance; she never danced. He was tall and lanky; she was very petite, probably just under five feet. Perhaps the opportunity to retreat to a "camp" on an island down the river and across the bay softened these differences. Snohomish was much less class-conscious than San Francisco, and "camp" was a further step toward informality and simplicity.

The story of their meeting and marrying is a popular family tale. Nina graduated from Oakland High School and received a certificate from a young ladies' seminary to teach school. She began teaching in Livermore, California, an area of dry, rolling hills and lush valleys east and south of Oakland.

In December of 1886, Nina's brother, Arthur, moved to Snohomish to work for the Blackman brothers, their father's cousins, in their general store. One of the Blackman brothers, Hyrcanus, was active on the school board and wrote to Nina, offering her a position of primary teacher in the grammar school commencing in February of 1887. The offer was for $45 or $50 a month and a chance for a raise. A second letter from Arthur encouraged Nina with the words, "I like the place first rate . . . there are a good many stumps but that doesn't matter. They ought to call this place Blackman City there are so many of them here."[3] The teaching offer and her brother's encourage-

> "My father's tales were peppered with words from the Chinook jargon. 'Skookum' meant strong and vigorous. 'Cultus' was the word for lazy."
>
> —Frances Bakeman Hodge

ment persuaded Nina, and her parents, that she should come to Snohomish.

Nina arrived on the steamer and, as church bells summon the faithful to prayer, the blast of the whistle gathered the town to the wharf. Among the faithful was Charles and, as he watched Nina disembark, he uttered the most quoted words in our whole family history, "I'm going to marry her and buy her a sky-blue dress to match her eyes."[4]

In an unfinished novel based on her mother Nina's early life in Snohomish, Frances Bakeman Hodge describes how she imagined the scene as Nina stepped off the steamer.

> "[Nina] . . . seemed fragile in figure and pastel in color. Her cream-colored hair under the soft pearl gray bonnet was like the finely spun curls of a young child. Her features and skin were soft and child like too, but the expression in her blue eyes was not that of an immature girl. She returned the curious scrutiny of the people on the dock with the calm glance of a poised woman. It was this combination of delicacy and composure that immediately intrigued [Charles]."[5]

Nina and Charles were married on June 20, 1887 in the front parlor of her cousin Alanson Blackman's home on Avenue B in Snohomish. Within a few months Nina and Charles were on a steamer to Oakland, where her parents gave a formal reception for the newly wed couple.

On their return to Snohomish Charles and Nina nestled into their first home. Their marriage began with an apparently prosperous first five years. Inez Mildred, my grandmother, was born on December 19, 1889. Two years later Guy joined the family. A gap of almost nine years before any more children were born coincided with a period of business setbacks and financial troubles for Charles. A fire at his store burned most of his business, and the insurance company refused to pay for the loses. Charles' losses of building and goods were estimated at $17,500. Creditors were after him. The family lost their house and moved to a little rental cottage at 317 Avenue B.

The insurance company never paid Charles for his losses, but this vital young man rebounded into solvency. We don't know if Nina and Charles joined the other State of Mainers to flock to the joys of Clinton Beach during these hard times. Perhaps the free fish, clams, and other sea life from the beach augmented a scant food budget. In any event their hard times eased with the turn of the century and Charles and Nina began the second half of their family. Frances Louise arrived in 1900 and Charles Theodore (Ted) in 1903.

Charles and Nina purchased the little house on Avenue B in which they were living. It evolved, over the years, to a spacious nine-room home where they lived for the rest of their lives. Frances describes the house she grew up in, "The house on Avenue B was furnished with many New England antiques, but the extra lot on Avenue A was used for a garden, orchard, chicken yard and stable, a mini-farm, like the big farm where the Bakemans lived in Wisconsin."[6] Years later when Frances was straightening things in the attic at 317 Avenue B, she uncovered a sky-blue brocaded silk dress carefully saved among her mother's possessions.

Family life kept Charles and Nina busy, as a small settlement was making its beginnings down the Snohomish River and across Possession Sound on the east shores of Whidbey Island.

Demands of family and starting a new business limited Nina and Charles's ability to purchase their "camp" on Clinton Beach. Other members of the Blackman clan did make purchases, as did two other State of Maine families, the Knapps and the Burkes, around the beginning of the twentieth century.

The Bakeman family in 1898.

Left to right: Charles, Guy (age 7), Inez (age 9), and Nina.

Settlement farther north on Whidbey preceded by a couple of decades settlement of South Whidbey. In 1890 the county courthouse in Coupeville was completed. Also that year, the first issue of the Island's first newspaper was published. The following year the official census tallied 1,417 white residents on Whidbey.

The two decades surrounding the change of the century marked many inventions that greatly enhanced transportation. The first motor-driven boat using an engine based on the explosive principle appeared in 1891. This opened the way for smaller, privately owned, power driven boats. In 1902, the first automobile and the first road appeared. By 1925 cars were commonly used on the Island. The highways of the generations prior to 1900 were the waterways—rivers and the numerous passages of Puget Sound. After automobiles and roads made overland transportation easy and the launches and steamboats obsolete, the positioning of our cabin on an island gained a new significance. The transportation revolution must be responsible, at least in part, for the separate sanctuary feeling of travel to an island that we feel so deeply today.

Traveling across on a ferry to an island sets the stage for a transition from real life—a physical and emotional departure from responsibilities and duties—and becomes an invitation to play. This is how we summer folk differ from the permanent settlers.

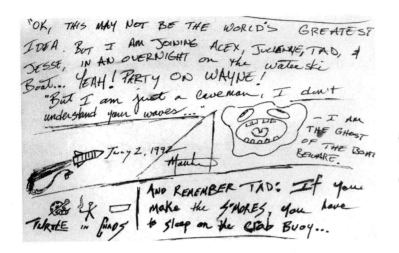

Cabin log entry, 1992. All ages enjoy creating a log entry.

Chapter 4

A 150-FOOT WATERFRONT LOT

"With growing prosperity the family bought a 150-foot waterfront lot on Whidbey Island where they came every summer for many years. At first everyone owning property at this beach were related in some way to the Blackman Brothers, cousins of Nina Blackman Bakeman, my mother. It had been the Blackman Brothers who had discovered the lovely beach in the first place."[1]

—Frances Bakeman Hodge

How and exactly when the Blackman brothers discovered the beach at Clinton has not been recorded, but I am not above making some assumptions. Being in the lumber business, they surely were aware of the logging going on down the Snohomish River and across the bay at the Hinman settlement on South Whidbey. The steamers that traveled up and down Saratoga Passage added stops at Island settlements after 1904. Prior to that there was no regular service, but numerous smaller boats, launches, could be hired to take passengers to designated areas. Early vacationers could have simply boarded a launch in Snohomish and traveled the whole distance by boat to Clinton beach. Smaller launches could come in close to shore; larger boats would use the Randall Point dock.

Randall Point, Clinton, in 1922. Salisbury shingle mill established in 1916 in center. Photo probably taken from roof of Clinton Dock.

Imagine the village of Clinton at about the turn of the century, centering around the dock and wharf at Randall Point. There was a store with post office and a hotel owned by Hinman. The surrounding area was homesteaded by several families. The beach settlement halted at a lagoon just north of the dock area. The marshy lagoon and slough prevented the town of Clinton from spreading northward, but did not prevent the summer folk from arriving by boat on the sandy beach across the lagoon.

Upland, the old-growth forests of fir and cedar were being cut and property full of stumps was selling quite cheaply for as low as $7 per acre. Improved and cleared land varied from $50 to $300 per acre. Clearing the stumps prior to farming was a difficult job but simplified by the use of explosive powder. An early business on the very southern end of Whidbey near Possession Point was a dock where barrels of explosive powder were brought in by boat, and a warehouse where the explosives were stored before being sold to farmers and businesses. This risky but profitable business became the perfect setting for a novel of intrigue and adventure as we will read later in the chapter called Beach Fiction.

Henry Hinman (the less adventurous brother who stayed in Clinton) owned 100 acres, including the land on the beach and along the bluff north of Randall Point beyond the lagoon. He logged the property and cleared his own homestead area for a small farm. From his crow's-nest viewpoint on top of the almost vertical bluff, Hinman enjoyed a spectacular view of the Cascade Mountain Range from Mt. Rainier toward the south to Mt. Baker directly across the bay. The southern tip of Camano Island was within view before it disappeared behind Sandy Point in the foreground. Hat Island sat like a squashed fedora in the middle of Possession Sound. With the aid of a captain's telescope, Hinman could watch the launches leave the mouth of the Snohomish River, travel across the bay, and deposit the happy campers onto his beach.

For some time the families from Snohomish camped and enjoyed the beaches and bounty without owning property. However, between 1902 and 1906 land on our section of the beach was officially purchased from Henry Hinman by members of the extended Blackman families, including the

Lenfest and Morgan families. Also, a 150-foot-wide section was purchased by two assumed-to-be unrelated families also from Snohomish, the Snyders and McCreadys.

The first record of a deed transfer from Henry Hinman to a Blackman occurred on April 12, 1903. Ella Blackman, the wife of Hyrcanus, purchased the lot. Ella was a Knapp, a member of one of the State of Maine pioneer families who helped settle Snohomish. Hyrcanus was the school board member who wrote to Nina in Oakland and offered her the teaching position in Snohomish. Having lived in the Snohomish area for 30 years, he was now well established and able to purchase land for recreation. Their two children, Clifford and Eunice, were in their late teens and early twenties.

A few months later, on August 16, a deed was recorded for the purchase of a lot by Eliza Howard Blackman, the wife of Alanson Blackman. Eliza and Alanson had offered their front parlor for the marriage of Charles and Nina 16 years earlier. Alanson, called Cap (short for Captain), probably had a boat at his disposal and was able to easily explore the south Whidbey area to look for property.

Three years later on December 26, 1906, a deed was recorded for the purchase of a lot by F. M. Blackman. Frances Blackman was the wife of a third Blackman brother, Elhanan. Frances's maiden name was Osgood.

It is interesting that all three deeds are in the wife's name only, rather than being purchased by both the husband and wife. Similarly, other early purchases along Clinton Beach were in the names of the women only. Present day lifestyles accept ownership by individuals within a marriage partnership. Conversely, in the early 1900s, this was a radically independent step for the women. The lots, and later the cabins, often were kept in the women's names and passed to daughters upon deaths of the owners. Perhaps it was the three sisters-in-law who first cherished and respected the beach as an oasis for their individual expression and as a refuge for creativity. Spending their days at home, rather than off at a job like their husbands, may have promoted a desire to get away to their beach property.

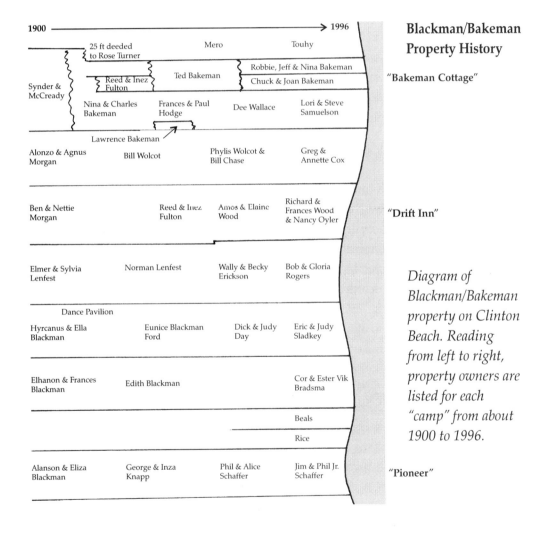

Blackman/Bakeman Property History

"Bakeman Cottage"

"Drift Inn"

Diagram of Blackman/Bakeman property on Clinton Beach. Reading from left to right, property owners are listed for each "camp" from about 1900 to 1996.

"Pioneer"

Then as now the inviting playground of the beach and all the adventures associated with beach living enthralled the children hour after hour and day after day. As the tide receded each day, the playground extended several hundred yards over the wide sandy tide flats. Children could explore the beach, wade in the shallow water, collect shells, and dig clams. Each day became a new self-directed treasure hunt. When the children are entertained, the mother's time becomes her own again. It opens the door to greater independence and creativity.

The wives of three of the Blackman brothers now owned their camps on Clinton Beach.[2] The Blackman brothers had an older sister, Mary Blackman Lenfest whose son, Elmer Lenfest, also purchased property during this time.[3]

On January 2, 1912, the deed was recorded that officially made our direct ancestors property owners on South Whidbey.

Many of the dates used thus far for exchange of property are recording dates—the date that a sale was recorded with the county. Land sales at the time were often agreed and acted upon long before they were recorded. Occasionally the recording was actually a correction of a deed, even with no record of the original sale. This was the case when, ten years after Snyder and McCready recorded their ownership deed, a deed was recorded indicating Nina and Charles Bakeman had purchased the 150-foot lot. This deed, however, is a corrected deed, with no reference to the original. It is not known exactly when Nina and Charley purchased the land—we suspect well prior to 1912.

Despite this blurry beginning, on January 2, 1912, the deed was recorded that officially made our direct ancestors property owners on South Whidbey. Nina not only followed her father's cousins to Snohomish, she also followed them down the river to camp.

While the extended Blackman clan settled their camps at the northern end of the original beach area, other State of Mainers settled closer to Randall Point, including the Knapp, Burke, and Clark clans. All four of these original beach families are related by marriage, which must have made for some great beach campfires.[4] Chuck Bakeman, grandson of Nina and Charles, has developed a "family tree" of the cabins showing the ownership of the cabins through the four generations. I have included it as an appendix beginning on page 115.

> "The cabins all had names like Shady Bereen, Camp Cozy, Camp Lew (that was Lew Clark's place, Pioneer, which [was on the site of] the Schaffer place, bought from the George Clarks by Phil Schaffer who is gone now, and who was my father's boyhood best friend.) There was Sharktooth Shoal which is gone now and HooRah's Nest. There also was The Temple of Purity. Everyone had a name to their tent or cabin which some people have kept but others are lost."[5]
> —*George Clark IV*

According to Margaret Clark Mykut, the practice of naming the camps came from the State of Maine. The families named their recreational properties in Maine and continued the practice here on Clinton Beach. "And they called it, 'going to Camp'."[6]

At one time the cabin belonging to Nina's daughter Frances Bakeman Hodge was called the Hodge Podge Lodge, an apt description of how the cabins were constructed. Simple camps grew from tent platforms, often built on top of beach logs. Later wooden walls and roofs replaced the tents. While excavating a septic system in the 1960s, Chuck Bakeman dug into a large drift log, still preserved, several feet under his side garden.

Both picnicking and dancing were popular forms of entertainment on South Whidbey well before our family purchased property. As early as 1887, a dance pavilion and waterfront camp ground were established at Glendale, just south of the present ferry dock.[7] A solidly built, enclosed dance hall was built for the permanent Clinton residents near the dock, which lured large numbers of visitors from the mainland to Whidbey for the weekends. At some point, probably in the 1910s, a dance pavilion was also built at the summer camp area of Clinton Beach. We know that Charles Bakeman loved to dance, and we can assume that the Blackman brothers also liked to kick up their heels since the open-air dance pavilion for the summer folk was located on property owned by Hyrcanus and Ella Blackman.[8] This more modest structure had a wooden floor and roof with open sides. A dock directly in front of the dance hall, which was shared by a half-dozen families near by, invited visitors to the dance festivities.

When Ella Blackman moved from Maine, she shipped her piano around Cape Horn and up the west coast to her new parlor in Snohomish. Both Ella and Hyrcanus must have recognized the importance of music to have endured the expense of moving the piano so far. They, perhaps, were the initiators of the music and dancing at the dance pavilion.

On summer evenings, as the full moon rises directly across the bay over the Cascades, the pathway of moon shimmer starts at Hat Island and glimmers across the flat water to end at our beach. With bellies full from a neighborhood clam bake and music drifting over the quiet bay, it is no wonder the families became intertwined.

By 1912, Nina and Charles's family of four had grown and changed. Inez, my grandmother, was 23 years old and about to be married the following year. Guy was 20 years old. Frances was 12 years old and the baby, Charles Theodore (Ted), an active nine-year-old.

Within a year of purchase of the 150 feet of waterfront, Nina and Charles deeded the north 25 feet to a Mrs. Rose Turner for $1. The official reason for the transfer is unclear. As the placement of tents and camping spaces often spread independent of official property lines, this may have simply brought the official ownership in line with agreed upon use and possession.

Oldest picture available of the Bakeman property at Clinton Beach in about 1910.

Gabled cabin in center was original structure owned by Nina and Charles (later replaced by Frances and Paul Hodge's house.) Camping tent on right is positioned where Reed built the cabin now called the Bakeman Cottage and owned by Chuck and Joan Bakeman.

My apologies for this vague photo, but it is the earliest picture of our family property at Clinton. It shows the original gable-roofed cabin possibly built by the original settlers, Snyder and McCready.[9] We assume that the parents, Nina and Charles, inhabited the cabin, with growing children and expanding family using the tents surrounding the cabin.

Sometime after the marriage of Inez to Horacio Reed Fulton in 1913, a cabin was built on the property to the north of the original cabin. That cabin, still very much its original size and shape, is presently owned by Chuck and Joan Bakeman. I grew up hearing the family story (which was recently corroborated by Harriet Fulton Putnam) that the cabin was given to Inez and Reed as a wedding present. More likely they were given the land and perhaps building materials, since other family stories report that Reed built the cabin.[10]

The use of the rest of the now 125-foot lot during these years can be assumed only by its subsequent division. Nina and Charles continued to occupy the original cabin, and Inez, the oldest offspring, the new cabin to the north. The next in line for a cabin would have been Guy, three years younger than Inez. Guy married in 1916 and produced one son, Lawrence, before Guy died in the influenza epidemic of 1919. The younger Bakeman children, Frances and Ted—being a half-generation younger—did not need cabins of their own until the 1920s.

House built by/for Reed and Inez after they were married in 1913. Inez is seated at left, shoeless Reed at right. The cabin is now owned by Chuck and Joan Bakeman.

We can imagine the idealistic summers at camp that Inez and Reed enjoyed, beginning with their marriage on June 20, 1913— exactly 26 years to the day after her parents, Nina and Charles, were married in the front parlor of Nina's cousin's house in Snohomish. Inez graduated from Snohomish High school on May 29, 1908, and attended Washington State College, where she graduated with a degree in music. "Always a lady," is how her nephew, Chuck Bakeman, described her. Inez's first grandchild, my brother Dick, started calling her Honey (after a toy bear named Honey Baby.) The name stuck, because Inez's disposition was sweet to the fiber of her being.

Reed graduated from high school in Asotin, Washington, in 1908 and also attended Washington State College. He dreamed of being a doctor, but gave that up and created a life of service to student's minds rather than their bodies. He taught school and wrote books to further stimulate young imaginations. Inez and Reed were both listed as residents of Snohomish at the time of the marriage. Their two daughters, Elaine (my mother) born in 1914 and Celeste born the following year, joined them for wonderful summers at the beach.

By the time the newlyweds first enjoyed their new cabin in 1913, the Clinton Union store, which had been built in 1904, was a thriving business. The original store started in the early 1880s and by the turn of the century, the expanding community had outgrown the early store and warranted a newer one, as this was the largest community in all of south Whidbey. The new store was located back from the Randall Point dock and carried an extensive line of merchandise for the permanent residents. A board sidewalk connected the store to the dock. Next to the dock was a waiting room and stable.

Reed Fulton cooling off with hat and newspaper.

At first the post office occupied just a cubby-hole in the store, but by 1920 a new building was built to house the post office. This was located on the beach north of the store. By this time a shingle mill built by Frank Salisbury was active as well.

The year 1919 brought the first car ferries to Clinton. That summer the 60-foot *Central* established a run from the old Clinton dock to Everett. A couple months later the *Whidbey*, a 59-foot gas-powered drive-through ferry, started its route between Mukilteo and the Phinney area. In 1923 another ferry, also called the *Whidbey* but twice as long with graceful lines carrying 25-35 cars and 400 passengers, started a run from Everett to Langley to Clinton. With the advent of the new larger ferries, a new ferry dock was constructed at Columbia Beach located about 3/4 of a mile south of the Randall Point dock. As auto traffic via the ferries became the popular mode of transportation, a change of Clinton's commerce center followed. In 1926 the Clinton Union Cooperative sold its building on the beach and built the new Clinton Union Store up the hill next to the road from the ferry. That move, from the steamer dock area to the top of the hill, signaled the beginning of the end of the trading center at Randall Point.

Fulton women in row boat in 1914.

Left to right: Grace and Lois Fulton (Reed's younger sisters), Inez Bakeman Fulton. Grace and Lois later purchased a cottage near the end of Brighton Beach Road.

While the family lived in Snohomish, the trip down to camp was a direct ride by launch down the river and across the bay. The trip across Possession Sound was not always uneventful. Years ago Frances Bakeman Hodge told the story to Chuck Bakeman's wife Joan about bringing a large, heavy cast-iron wood-burning cook stove from Snohomish across the bay by boat to "camp." The boat, presumably a launch, exited the mouth of the Snohomish River and headed northwest toward Whidbey. On the back side of Hat Island a big north wind picked

Old Clinton Union Store (left) established in 1903. Also, Salisbury home and Hastings Store. Across the road is the Salisbury Shingle Mill.

up and, as the boat rocked, the heavy stove began to thrash around, banging against the sides of the boat. The passengers were unable to keep the stove under control and became concerned for the safety of the boat and their lives. They made the decision to jettison the stove over the side. And down to the bottom of the deep blue sea it went.

During the 1920s, Reed and Inez established their home in Seattle and the trip to the beach changed. They drove to the Mukilteo ferry and boarded the ferry to Whidbey. Once on the island, they drove in from the south along the Old Clinton (now called Brighton Beach) Road. Cars were parked at the end of the road, which was stopped by the lagoon and slough. The old garages, one of which we still own, designated the end of the old Clinton Road. The community built a boardwalk across the lagoon to access the beach houses to the north. Once across the marshy area, belongings were hauled along the rough path in front of the cabins.

Harriet Fulton Putnam (niece of Inez and Reed), at age 14 in 1930, remembers very well the boardwalk. Her father was

Reed's brother, and Harriet's family often visited Reed Fulton and his family at their camp.

> "There was a boardwalk from the old garages beyond Salisbury's and past Aunt Lois's place, (when it was back). And I remember one time we had come over for a Sunday or some kind of celebration. Mother was preparing a pie and this boardwalk wasn't always kept-up and some how or other a board wasn't where it should have been and she dropped the pie. That was one thing I remember about the boardwalk more than anything else. It didn't have any sides, just a walk."[11]

Just prior to World War II, the Island County Commissioners agreed to undertake a rather ambitious project: to fill the slough and continue the road to its present terminus.

Since the year 1900, beach walkers and fishermen have used the brickyard of the Sandstone Brick and Lime Company (also

Clinton beach and dock at Randall Point from hill. Clinton Union Store and water tower at right, Salisbury Shingle Mill at left, Hat Island in the distance.

Chapter 4 A 150-FOOT WATERFRONT LOT

The steamer **Whidbey** *in about 1923. This boat should not be confused with the early gas-powered ferry or the larger steam-powered ferry of the same name.*

called the Northwest Brick and Lime Company) as a landmark. Now a jumble of concrete slabs and old pilings jutting out of the sand at low tide, it offers a mini-ecology of pools full of barnacles, muscles, China hats, and those little multi-colored crab that scurry away when their rock-home is turned over. Tiny fish get trapped when the tide goes out in the old foundation, which now forms aquarium pools. The fingerlings hide in the cool shade but dart off when disturbed. The Brickyard is located about 1/4 mile north of our cabin and marks the last beach house before the land shakes free of development and opens to deserted meandering and quiet meditative reflection.

When Nina and Charles first started coming "down to camp" and set out for a beach walk going north, they passed undeveloped shore before approaching this flourishing plant. The main office of the company was in Seattle. Pressed brick were produced at this location from 1900 to 1916 under the direction of Guy Smith and his brother. Using the gray-blue native sand gathered from the same cliffs where we carve our initials and hydrated lime, they produced a sandlime brick hardened by pressure in a steam autoclave. This brick appeared in fireplaces and chimneys along the beach, but the soft sandy texture of the product prevented the business from being a lasting success. After the Sandstone Brick and Lime Company closed in 1916, it was a temptation for the young people on the beach to explore. George Clark IV remembered, "Yes, I used to play in that place . . . If they caught us we'd get hell. I don't remember the old hotel that went with the brick place." [12]

Chuck Bakeman does remember the old hotel.

The abandoned Brickyard and hotel buildings in 1930.

Left to right: Celeste, Margery, Elaine, and Helen Fulton. Margery and Helen were cousins of Elaine and Celeste.

"In the 1930s and 1940s the abandoned Brickyard and adjacent hotel was a hulk with great attraction for youngsters to climb on. The more daring would scramble to the top, three stories above ground, and venture out on beams without visible means of support. All who partook in such adventure would admit that if their mother knew what they had done they would be grounded for the remainder of the summer."[13]

The original fireplace and chimney of our cabin used this brick. The sandy quality of the brick caused it to break down and weather. Before we removed the chimney and fireplace, replacing them with an efficient wood-burning stove during the remodel of 1983, one could see daylight through the back of the fireplace where the brick had severely weathered.

Inez's youngest brother Ted always said fishing was good off the Brickyard. He said there was a nice deep hole where the fish hid out, just waiting for a tidbit. I put this off to fishing lore since the sand, at low tide, took its regular course of following in a parallel offshore line the high tide shoreline. Within the last few years, the cycles of drifting sands and seas have revealed stumps of pilings leading from the Brickyard down a steepish beach. At low tide the beach now makes a dramatic turn from its typical meandering parallel to the shore, and carves out a semi-circular bay as it probably did in the past. Fishing is now severely restricted in the best of years but, I bet, if the fish do return, they'll be catching them again at the pothole off the Brickyard.

Ted's son, Chuck Bakeman, must have been listening to his father when fishing lore was discussed. Here is his theory behind the fishing holes.

> "Salmon like to congregate in pockets of deeper water where a hole exists or where the bottom starts to slope down a bar. My Dad believed that one reason for this is that the fish like to lie in wait for bait, such as candle fish or herring, to pass over them carried by the current. When bait passes over, the salmon rapidly swim up to feed. The action of fishing lures, including candle fish or herring on a hook, is designed to give the motion of a wounded or dying bait to attract the salmon from the depts."[14]

Reed and Inez Fulton in 1925.

Walking the beach either north to the Brickyard or if very energetic as far as Sandy Point or south to the Randall Point dock or perhaps the ferry dock has consumed countless recreational beach hours. Walking at low tide offers wide sandy beaches, sea weeds, cockles, pools of water with sand shrimp, whereas the same beach at high tide is rocky, with driftwood, possible beachcombing treasures, and perhaps agates. A windy day, a cloudy day, or a light drizzle, can alter the same walk from one day to another. An almost infinite variety of beach walks is possible, as the beach—as well as my attitude—changes and filters the experience.

Another popular walk during the 1930s, according to Harriet Fulton Putnam, was the walk to Deer Lake. This small park-sized lake is located 1-1/3 miles west of Randall Point. A small community had sprung up there when Clinton was first settled. The first school in the Clinton area was established at Deer Lake just prior to 1900. Later, in 1915, a new modern school was built.

Deer Lake is also the source of the refreshing river that had attracted Hinman to settle in this spot in the first place. In 1928 a hydroelectric plant was built at the outflow of Deer Lake, moderating the flow of the river and supplying water to service the growing community around the Lake. The cascading river, which carved the ravine connecting Old Clinton and the budding business area up the hill, was reduced to a simple stream. A walk along the beach today reveals nothing of the stream, which now is piped under the road and discharges into the bay well below mean low tide.

During the late 1920s, I imagine "camp" getting quite cozy with three budding families and the grandparents, Nina and Charles, still active and vital. Reed was about to publish his first book and, with summers dedicated to that pursuit, needed a quiet place to write. I'm sure Inez and Reed noticed that their neighbor, Nettie Morgan Taylor, two houses to the south—since becoming a widow and remarrying—infrequently used her house. Perhaps they discussed how delightful it would be to occupy that larger, two-story space.

The year 1930 was poised to be a year of change for the Fulton family at Clinton Beach.

Cabin log entry, 1980. "We'd rather be here than anywhere else," reflects our continual love affair with the cabin.

Chapter 5

CAMP ILLAHEE

The word *illahee* comes from the indigenous languages of the Pacific Northwest. Meaning earth, ground, land, country, place, or world—and sharing its root in the Chinook language with *tillicum* (people, relative, friend)—*illahee* carries a sense of home, and of connections between people and living place.[1]

While the Blackman clan occupied several lots to the south and the growing Bakeman family enjoyed their 150 feet (now reduced to 125 feet) to the north, the Morgan brothers, Ben Sr. and Alonzo, created their camps on two lots in the middle. Ben

On August 13, 1902, Nettie and Ben Morgan, along with two other couples, hired a launch to look for a summer camp.

and Nettie Morgan, who purchased their lot from Hinman in 1902, decided to call their property Camp Illahee. This name came not from Maine, where many of the camp names had originated, but from Northwest Indian jargon. Ben Morgan was a native of Washington Territory, born in Olympia in 1864. This may explain why he chose a name from the Indian heritage for his camp; he had no personal ties with Maine as did his beach neighbors.

Illahee portrays the honor people feel for a beautiful place and the connection of place, land, ground to friends and relatives. Even though the name *Illahee* was dropped when the land came into our family as a result of its sale to Reed and Inez Fulton, the sense of land as sacred and the connections between people and a place are as strong as ever. Camp Illahee is a spectacularly beautiful setting, but it is the tradition of family—five generations on the same beach—that makes it a unique and powerfully attractive sanctuary.

As mentioned in the last chapter, all of the beach and hillside north of the settlement at Randall Point was originally owned by Henry C. Hinman. Nettie and Ben Morgan were the next owners of the land where our cabin was built (Camp Illahee.) Ben Morgan and his brothers owned the Pioneer Mill in Snohomish, which later was renamed the Morgan Bros. Mill. Ben was elected to the state legislature after statehood was established in 1889. Ben and Nettie were married in 1885; a year later Maude arrived and in 1889 Ben Jr. joined the family. Maude later married Clifford Blackman, son of Hyrcanus and Ella Blackman who had their beach camp just two lots south.

On a sunny summer day on August 13, 1902, Nettie and Ben Morgan, along with two other couples, hired a launch to look for a summer camp. One of the couples was Ben's brother

Alonzo Morgan and his wife Agnus. The other couple was Elmer and Sylvia Lenfest. (Elmer Lenfest was a Blackman progeny since his mother was Mary Blackman Lenfest, the older sister of the three Blackman Brothers who helped found Snohomish.) Nettie and Ben Morgan chose the lot our family later purchased. Alonzo and Agnus Morgan selected the lot to the north, and Elmer and Sylvia Lenfest selected the lot to the south. Deeds were recorded for the sale of the three properties from Hinman to Ben Morgan, Alonzo Morgan, and Elmer Lenfest indicating a sale of property on August 13, 1902. It is assumed this is the date spoken of in the following letter from Nettie Morgan to Inez Fulton.

Sources have not left an account of how Nina and Charles Bakeman first discovered their camp, but we have a delightful account of how Nettie and Ben Morgan discovered and purchased Camp Illahee for $25 at about the same time. Nettie Morgan's letters to Inez Fulton reach back to the Morgan's first summer visit to the property.

> "As perhaps you remember, Ben and Lon [Alonzo] hired a launch many years ago, and, with Agnus, Sylvia and myself—started on a cruise to find a permanent camping ground—by chance we stopped at Clinton and Dallas Salisbury directed us to the present camping place. At that time the lot we bought was the most desirable from our point of view—the one Agnus chose suited her best as it had more trees on it.
>
> "Lon went up on the hill and got Mr. Hinman to come down and see us—at the time Ben was almost a cripple—just recovering from a broken

leg and could not climb the hill—and then and there, we purchased our camp sites. Sylvia and Elmer buying next, then the Blackmans and later the others.

"Everything looked so beautiful at our place, water coming down off the hill—a nice dry place and white clover growing over it."[2]

Camp Illahee later called Drift Inn in 1914. Camp Illahee is in the center with the flag. To the left is the Lenfest house, to the right are the storage shed (behind) then Alonzo Morgan's house.

Three decades later Nettie Morgan had become Mrs. D. M. Taylor and was living in Wenatchee. It was there that Inez Fulton addressed her letters when she and her husband Reed pondered the purchase of Camp Illahee, or what is now called Drift Inn. Through the fall of 1929 and early part of 1930, several chatty letters crossed between Nettie Morgan Taylor and Inez Fulton where they discussed their children's activities, health of family members, and the purchase of Camp Illahee. The only letters in our possession are the ones from Nettie to Inez, from which I have quoted liberally below. The letters portray Nettie and Inez as quite personal and familiar, their having been neighbors both on the beach and in Snohomish. Nettie's daughter

Maude was now the widow of Clifford Blackman (son of Hyrcanus and Ella Blackman), who had died rather young in the flu epidemic of 1920. Nettie and her new husband had decided to build a new cabin at different location with easier access, and had not used Camp Illahee recently. Nettie noted, "[she] had not been there for so many years [she] did not know how it looks at this time."[3] Evidently the camp was being used by Nettie's children Ben Morgan and Maude Blackman and their families.

"After talking to Ben (presumed to be Nettie's son, Ben Jr.) in regards to the Clinton property, I have decided to take $1,200 for it. Ben says the bulkhead is all gone and he thinks $150 would put a new one in."[4] The letter continues with much discussion about the water source, where the stream originates, and who has use of it. The stream ran on "our property near the north line with quite a large flow of water. . . Lon [Alonzo Morgan, brother of Ben, who owned the lot to the north] always piped his water from our place."

The Fultons countered with an offer of $1,100, which prompted these words from Nettie in her following letter, "It nearly took my breath away to think of selling my place so cheap." Further on in the same letter she accepts the offer. Inez and Reed sent a down payment check for $300, which was returned with a request for $500. (Nettie needed more cash to build her new cabin.) Nettie's next letter ends with these words, "I am glad you are going to have our dear old place instead of strangers— and—may you always have the wonderful times there, that we have had."[5] Evidently by the summer of 1930 Inez and Reed had full use of the cabin. The contract called for an additional payment of $300 in March of 1931 and again in March of 1932, at which time they became full owners.

Nettie Morgan Taylor gives an imaginative description of the main house at Camp Illahee in a letter discussing the purchase. "The house was built by J. S. White and that means it could be rolled over and over and not come to pieces—and—between the three buildings there is lots of good lumber. It is not just the value of the lumber, but getting it delivered on the ground, that is a great burden."[6] The three buildings referred to are the main cabin and two extra guest cottages, one on each side of the main cabin. Not mentioned but a necessity was the outhouse located next to the bank near the south property line.

The mention of J. S. White as the builder of Camp Illahee was a positive selling point because he had long ago established himself in Snohomish as a well-respected architect and builder. Often the cabins along the beach just grew amorphously from log tent-platforms-with-sides to enclosed cabins. Camp Illahee, it appears, was designed and built with intention. J. S. White's New England rearing influenced his trade, and one can just as easily imagine our cabin sitting on a rocky Maine coast as snuggled under the bluff here on Clinton Beach. The *Snohomish Sun*, in January 1891, described the builder as follows:

> "J. S. White, the well known architect and builder, is a native of New Hampshire, and learned his trade in the city of Topeka. He came to Snohomish early in 1884, and has been engaged ever since in building and contracting. He is the architect and builder of nearly every building of note in the city. Among the residences built by him are those of E. C. Ferguson, O. C. Crossman, Mrs. Sinclair, H. C. Comegys, H. C. Morgan, etc., etc. Among the business blocks and fittings put up by him are

Wilbur's Burns, A. M. Blackman's, Otten's Store, Burton and Thornton, Plaskett's Hotel, part of the Blackman Block, Methodist Church and many others."[7]

Morning ritual in about 1927. Donna MacKenzie Bakeman (Ted's wife) and siblings Max, Janet, and Sarah in front of Ted Bakeman's camp.

Nettie's letter continues, "A few years later we found the spring on Elmer's [Lenfest] place free of sand and we began to use drinking water from his well, but, had our spring piped to our back door for other purposes. The little flume between our place and Elmer's was built to carry the water off. Also the one by the side of Maude's little cabin [to the north]. Those two flumes were supposed to be nearly on the [property] lines."[8]

We have not discovered a date when the cabins were built, but since generous use of the Brickyard bricks was incorporated into the original fireplace and chimney, we conclude that the construction was prior to the Brickyard closure in 1916. J. S. White died in October of 1920, supporting the estimate that our cabin, which still stands, was built in the early 1910s.

In June of 1930, within months of purchasing Camp Illahee, Reed and Inez also purchased the hillside behind the cabin to protect and control the spring, which was the water source for the cabin. They paid $25 to Mr. Hinman for the bank up to the county road. The county road referred to is the Old Hinman Road, now vacated, which was located just along the crest of the bluff (not the present Bob Galbreath Road, which basically runs parallel to the Old Hinman Road, much farther away from the bluff).

A year later, in May of 1931, Reed and Inez purchased a 50' x 10' garage near the end of Brighton Beach Road. Elmer Lenfest charged $1 for the garage and easement for driving over and across the 30 feet in front of the garage. These purchases were added to the 100' x 164' (34/100 acre) lot and bank as well as the tidelands already in their possession. The tidelands in front of Camp Illahee were purchased by Elmer Lenfest from the State of Washington and deeded to Ben Morgan in May of 1908. Elmer, being a surveyor and trained in recording of plats, provided this service to many of the cabin owners in 1908.

Further letters with Nettie Morgan Taylor and Elmer Lenfest reveal that the position of the south property line was under discussion. The edge of Elmer Lenfest's house was positioned five feet on the now Fulton property. Elmer proposed to lease the land until he could afford to purchase it or move his house. "Will you please let me know if it will be satisfactory to you to lease the 5 feet to me for, say 5 years at a nominal rental with the privilege of buying for $50 if at any time before the expiration of the lease I so desire. I have two things to consider in the proposition to move; my house is too low and by moving I could get a little out of the path of probable slides."[9] A five-year lease arrangement at $5.00 per year with option to purchase for $50 was agreed to and recorded in February of 1931. I have not found the recorded documents indicating a sale was consummated. However, I expect they exist knowing the very thorough and business-like nature of Reed.

When Inez and Reed purchased Camp Illahee, it eased the burden for her parents Nina and Charles of deciding how to divide up their 125 feet of waterfront among their four adult children. As soon as they purchased Camp Illahee, Reed and Inez sold their original cabin to Inez's younger brother, Ted, for "$10 and other goods and valuable considerations." Nina and Charles then deeded the middle 48 feet of property with a cabin to their daughter Frances. The last offspring, Guy, had died several years before, but Nina and Charles wanted Guy's son Lawrence to have an interest and gave him the remaining 20 feet. Later Lawrence traded his 20 feet to Frances for room and board while he attended the University of Washington.

Reed's occupation as a teacher and principal allowed the family the luxury of packing up and moving to the beach for the summer. Given their busy social life and demands on Reed during the school year, I surmise this retreat became a welcome reprieve. They rented out their Seattle home to teachers coming to the University of Washington for the summer. Ted's family and Frances's family also moved over to the beach for the summer. If needed, fathers would commute on the weekends, but moms and kids enjoyed a fun-filled summer on the beach.

The beach life continued as a welcome break from city life for women during the 1930s. The beach represented a haven of

Three cousins in their newly made shorts, walking along the elevated boardwalk constructed over the marshy lagoon to connect the row of summer camps and the town of Old Clinton.

Left to right: Elaine Fulton, cousins Harriet and Margery Fulton.

DOWN TO CAMP: A History of Summer Folk on Whidbey Island

informality and close interaction with extended family and with nature. By then the strict mores of the late Victorian period were replaced with bobbed haircuts, loose-fitting clothing, and, finally, trousers. Harriet Fulton Putnam remembers getting a new sewing machine and sewing her first pair of shorts for the beach.

"The guy-thing to do in the early 1930s was definitely fishing," explained Chuck Bakeman. "Back then you really caught fish! There was a major salmon run up the Snohomish River and it was not unusual to catch a couple 10- to 30-pound king salmon on a weekend."[10] Speculation on salmon runs, the best lures, and places where salmon hung out were hot topics of conversation.

Two particularly dependable fishing holes were the bar off the south end of Hat Island and at the Shell dock. When the runs of salmon moved to different waters the fishermen drove to Double Bluff or Possession Point, rented a boat there and went fishing. If fishing from a rowboat, the Shell Dock or the pot hole opposite the Brickyard were the best destinations.

Chuck remembers how impressed he was as a boy with his uncle Reed's boat.

> "All the men-folk were fisherman on the beach and had boats but Reed's boat was one of the finest. It was a very sturdy wooden boat 17-18 feet long, very heavy, and painted red. I always felt very safe being in his boat because it was big and sturdy. Reed was one of the first on the beach to have an outboard motor. Prior to that, the boats were smaller and we rowed. The engine on Reed's boat had a handle on the

flywheel which was cranked to start the engine. This was state-of-the-art technology for outboard motors replacing having to pull the rope wound around the flywheel. Reed's engine had five or six horse power—perfect for trolling and fishing."[11]

Family on steps of original Bakeman cottage in about 1930. Notice the board pathway, allowing owners to walk from the road-end to their cabins. This pathway, now mostly concrete, is still used today.

Left to right, back row: Reed Fulton, unknown, Grace Fulton
Front row: Inez Fulton, Lois Fulton, and Elaine Fulton.

When ferry traffic took over transportation needs, the dock at Randall Point was purchased by Shell Oil. Oil was off-loaded into a warehouse on the dock and then distributed. Kids enjoyed fishing from the old Shell Dock. The perch that fed on the pilings could easily be lured onto a hook. Chuck remembers one afternoon catching literally a wheelbarrow full of piling perch. He wheeled them home, much to Chuck's mom's surprise. She responded kindly and Chuck still remembers her innovative response, "We'll bury them under the rose bush on the south side." Chuck recalls the next year they had the biggest healthiest roses ever.

Another time, while fishing off the old Shell Dock, Chuck remembers the Chicken Boat's arrival. Actually it was the *Virginia V* docking with its hold full of live chickens.

While the men were off fishing, the women kept busy making preserves and canning. Chuck remembers this activity during the mid to late 1930s. Since the families spent the summer at the beach, the duty of making summer preserves transferred from town to the beach. Sugar and canning supplies were purchased at Randall Point where Guy Smith ran a general store and post office. The jars of brightly colored bulk candy lined up in a row on the counter were just at eye level for young Chuck as he followed his mother for supplies. Apples were available locally and applesauce was stewed and canned. As a child I remember a large cherry tree just south of the Hodge property. Wild blackberries were plentiful along the road and up the bank, and berry-picking was a typical family outing in the late summer. Today the blackberries have invaded the bank and rooted themselves just 30 feet from our back door.

Raub was in the house asleep when he and the house were lifted off its foundation and pushed nearly to the bay.

Harriet Fulton Putnam remembers Mrs. Hastings, a Clinton resident up the hill, who recognized the summer folk as a market for her extra garden produce. Mrs. Hastings carried a basket of vegetables to sell along the beach cabins. She always came to the back door—where the kitchens were then located—looking for the cooks.

The most devastating slides on South Whidbey have occurred at Possession Point as the southwest winds and waves continue to eat away at that southern-most exposed tip of the Island. Massive slides occurred in 1910, 1949, and 1979. Five acres of bluff property dropped off in 1949 burying several beach cottages below. Another area that has suffered slide damage is our own Clinton Beach, although to a much lesser degree than the Possession Point disasters. Our bluff slips and slides almost every winter when the heavy rains saturate the hill and bring down mud and brush as it settles into backyards. On three or four occasions in the 90-some years our family has been visiting the beach, the slides have destroyed homes. One area particularly susceptible to sliding is the bluff between Camp Illahee and the Bakeman Cottage.

The earliest first-hand story of a slide comes from Inez's sister, Frances Bakeman Hodge. Hers is the story of a tree charging in the back door and sticking out the front described earlier. That may have been the reason a newer house was built on that property in about 1928, replacing the original cabin used by Nina and Charles. The newer one is the peaked roof house with the stone fireplace, used for many years by Frances and Paul Hodge (Hodge Podge Lodge). According to Chuck Bakeman, in about 1950 a slide clipped a new kitchen off the house that stuck out to the south. That section of the bluff, however, remained relatively quiet for forty years until shortly after the Samuelsons purchased the house and remodeled it. In 1990 a devastating slide deposited the house over the bulkhead and into the bay. Then, five years later, as an afterthought, a slide dislodged the tower room behind the Bakeman Cottage.

Harriet Fulton Putnam has in her scrapbook a news article from the Everett Daily Herald telling of the slide around 1933 that occurred closer to Camp Illahee. On Friday, January 24 of that year, the rains became the heaviest ever recorded, and the hillside behind the house just to the north of Reed and Inez's main cabin let go with vengeance. The lot, which had been settled by Alonzo Morgan, brother of Ben Morgan Sr., was now owned by W. W. Wolcott. His new house, built just two years prior to the slide, was rented by Lincoln Raub. Raub was in the house asleep when he and the house were lifted off its foundation and pushed nearly to the bay. He escaped unharmed and with quite a tale to tell. That slide also spread onto the property of

Camp Illahee and demolished the guest cottage to the north of our main house. A much smaller slide occurred in the same area about 1986, causing minor damage but spreading mud and brush to a thickness of four feet to the north of the cabin.[12]

Slides are a phenomenon of the rainy winter months and are soon forgotten with the warm sunny days of summer. Free, unstructured days provide time and opportunity for pursuing creative goals. The cabin has long been a haven for writing, painting, creative projects, or just puttering. Reed combined the free time of the summer months with the romantic setting of south Whidbey to create the first of his many published novels. In the next chapter we will explore beach fact, fiction, and myth.

> 7/23, 24, 25/93 — THE GREAT SEPTIC ADVENTURE
> Cathy & Dick just make the Midnight ferry on Friday. Saturday is POURING! We WAIT FOR THE RAIN TO stop AND the diggers to Arrive. By 3:00 pm, the rain has stopped but NO Oylers. So A Quick dash to Langley to pick up Cathy's ring which LIND was re-sizing. Back at 5:00 & VOILÁ!! The grass is cut & the septic tank & drain field exposed & Oyler's playing cards with grins of SATisfaction on the bulkhead. The digging continues; the pipe is "hosed" (Julienne — "I'm never using that hose again!" The Tool does A triple FLUSH & water comes out the pipe! What remains to be done is dig out a drain basin & fill with gravel.

Cabin log entry, 1993. Adventures can be fictional, as in Reed's books, or real life, as with our fickle septic system.

Chapter 6

BEACH FICTION

At the extreme southern point of Whidbey Island, the Possession Point bluff flares out slightly to form a protective barrier... Located there was the famous (or infamous, depending on who is discussing it) Giant Powder Works, which was immortalized in the well known novel written by Reed Fulton, *The Powder Dock Mystery*.[1]

Reed's niece, Harriet Fulton Putnam, remembers that the rules were clear when visiting the cabin; if Reed was writing the children had to be quiet, especially around the little cabin to the south. Camp gave Reed time and space for pursuing his writing career and a rich natural setting to enliven his imagination.

Two of Reed's early books, *The Powder Dock Mystery,* copyrighted in 1927, and the *Tide's Secret,* which followed in 1930, were set in and around south Whidbey. I can imagine Reed composing these words from the *Powder Dock Mystery* while sitting on the cabin porch early in the morning:

> "The horizon clouds above the blue-black ridge of the Cascades had decked themselves in grayest orange in honor of the coming of the sun. Upon the quiet waters of the Sound lay a fainter reflection of the approaching splendor. Two mud hens were busy with the morning feeding not far from shore; their soft quacking was barely audible. A blue crane, intent on better feeding grounds, flapped slowly past just above the water, his hoarse 'krank krank' a reminder of solemn things."

Reed spent his adult life working with high school students and identified a significant gap in the teaching of literature and language arts to this age group. The accepted literature of the day was written for adults. Reed observed that students benefited from literature written for their age and interests. He dedicated much of his time to writing the novels himself. He wrote about young people trying to make a living for themselves, but running into adventure and mystery along the way. In *The Powder Dock Mystery,* the hero is employed at the Powder Dock Company. He and his sister try to solve the mystery of the man in the fish scale mask who is threatening them. Living under the fear that the Powder Dock could be sabotaged at any minute keeps the suspense alive.

Reed continued his writing with *Lardy the Great*, which explored the theme of being an overweight teenager. *Stevedore* was based on his personal experience working on the wharves of Seattle during two summers of World War II. *Grand Coulee Mystery* followed the building of the Grand Coulee Dam over the Columbia River in Eastern Washington. The pioneer western movement is explored in *The Moccasin Trail*.

My grandfather, Reed Fulton, author, at his roll-top desk.

His publisher, Doubleday, snatched up his stories as soon as they were completed. Judging from the amount of public speaking he was asked to do, as is documented in his daily journal entries between the years 1942 and his death in 1957, he was a well-respected Seattle author.

Reed was not the only relation to find the beach conducive to creativity. His two maiden sisters, Lois and Grace Fulton, purchased a cabin near the end of Brighton Beach Road in 1936. Lois, a painter and art teacher, spent the summer pursuing her creativity at the beach. Recently their former cabin was scheduled for demolition and the present owners suggested that I take a look through the old tower room studio. Paintings, drawings, masks, even a wind vane were discovered. Lois, it seems, couldn't stop painting. She decorated the back concrete retaining wall from top to bottom with a garden full of plants and flowers. Grace was a weaver and home economics teacher. Finely woven mats, also uncovered in the tower room, were remnants of her craft.

The stillness and lack of schedule demands at the beach have allowed many of us to revisit a creative self we left back in our sand castle stage.

The stillness and lack of schedule demands at the beach have allowed many of us to revisit a creative self we left back in our sand castle stage. For Reed it was writing fiction, the Fulton Aunts painted and wove, and Frances Bakeman Hodge wrote historical fiction. These relations left tangible evidence of their creativity. For others the product has not survived, but the personal benefit always remains in the soul of the creator. Fashioning a feast of seafood fresh from the bay followed by berry pie picked behind the cabin can give satisfaction to both the creators and the consumers. Today we stash paints and brushes at the cabin for decorating clam shells or (a rather new art form for us) painting patterns on long beach sticks—shaman style.

"You can do what you want at camp." What an invitation for creativity! Just imagine the original Blackman wives and Nina as they left the strict mores of the Victorian life in Snohomish and escaped to the freedoms of beach living. Here they could lift their skirts and wade in the cool waters of Possession Sound, don a bathing costume, or run shoeless on the beach. We have no record of their creative endeavors, but I'd bet they were numerous.

Reed's fiction wasn't the only story-telling going on at the cabin. Most families have a myth maker, an old codger or crone who, with a hidden twinkle in his or her eye, loves to astound the younger generation with stories, tall tales, and fudged truths.

In our family it was my great-uncle Ted. Looking through the table of contents of the *South Whidbey and its People*, I noticed a chapter on fishing with records of the biggest fish caught on South Whidbey. Here, I figured, even though we have always been just summer folk, we would surely be mentioned. I had known from the time I could speak the word "fish," that my own Uncle Ted was the undisputed champion fisherman of the area. I knew that as a fact, *because he had told us.*

According to the history book, the biggest fish ever was a 58-pound king salmon caught by Les Bennett just south of Clinton. No second place, not even a mention of Uncle Ted! If he were here to defend himself, I can just see that twinkle in his eye and hear his newest myth. "Oh, it isn't the biggest fish that is important, it's the largest number of fish. I remember, back before there were fishing licenses and restrictions on the number you could haul out of the wulge,[2] I remember . . . the fish were so thick you could almost walk on their backs all the way across to . . . "

If the old adage is true that the greatest amount of time spent fishing produces the most fish, then the following tale about Uncle Ted, told to me by his youngest son, Jeff, may be the secret to Ted's fishing success. "I remember after we moved up from California and Dad had a job in Everett, he would commute by boat. Dressed in his suit and tie, he rolled up his pants, and roared away from shore going south."[3] Jeff remembers hearing, from his bed in the still dawn hours, the engine drop to a troll as Ted got to the old Shell Dock. He fished through that section and then roared off to the boathouse in Everett where he left his boat, often with fish in the bottom. After work Ted picked up the boat and retraced his path, stopping to fish again at the old Shell Dock on his way home.

Another family story with larger-than-life deeds is a story my brother remembers about our mother Elaine (with her father Reed) rowing a boat around Whidbey Island in a day. I had assumed this was all myth until I posed the question to Chuck Bakeman. He said, "Oh, but she did! Actually it took two days and she and her dad had the help of a motor."

"That was during the time that fathers took their offspring for adventures together," he continued. "Reed, Elaine's father, had a large sturdy boat. It was red with a fancy new motor." Elaine and Reed packed up early one morning, checked the tides and the flow through Deception Pass at the north end of Whidbey Island, and started out. They motored all of one day and camped somewhere on the west side of the Island. By the end of the second day, they had circumnavigated the second longest island in the lower 48 states.

Chuck picked up the thought again. "It was me and my father (Ted) who did the rowing!" However, their destination was Hat Island located directly in the center of Possession Sound between our beach, Everett, and Camano Head. The plan was to row to Hat Island, camp there one night, and row back. Their mode of transportation was much more humble, an eight-foot dingy. It was round-bottomed, with a painted and sealed canvas stretched on the wooden frame. The father-and-son team packed tent, axes, and food, and set off into the freshening afternoon breeze. Judging from how scared he became when the wind picked up, Chuck estimated he must have been about five years old at the time. As the waves got larger and the current stronger, Ted commanded Chuck to sit in the bottom of the boat to add some stability. "A huge wind picked up and I remember looking *up* at the waves, and it was very scary." In hindsight Chuck judged the crossing to be life-threatening.

Father and son made the beach and camped near the old gravel pit. A large derelict wooden structure remained, which at one time was used to move the gravel from up on the hill to barges waiting at the dock. They fell into a sound sleep, glad to be on solid ground. In the black of night a light flashing in their faces awakened them. " A man with a wolf-like dog was standing over them." He was the watchman from the old gravel pit checking the beach for fugitives. Convinced of their innocent adventure, the watchman gave permission for them to camp. In the morning they had an uneventful row home.

One story we wish were true is the rumor that there were geoducks along this beach. An early promotion for visitors to a resort at Maple Cove, south of Sandy Point, described these delicious clams as being available for digging at the resort. Geoducks are a large bivalve with a long thick siphon or neck. The clam itself lives deep in the sand and extends the siphon up 2-3 feet to the surface of the sand. You don't *dig* geoducks, that word is too passive, you *catch* geoducks. Catching a geoduck is a real challenge since the siphon can quickly disappear below the surface of the sand and the clam itself can dig deeper if disturbed. I posed the geoduck rumor to Chuck.

The geoduck, a large bivalve clam, was once collected along Clinton Beach at low tide.

"I'm sure that in about 1955 on a real low tide I walked way out in front of the Fulton cabin and actually saw a very large siphon. I had been taught to drive a thin sharp stick in sideways to pierce the neck and hold the neck from going down." Chuck recently carefully examined the same spot at low tide and found no trace of the bivalve.

This myth could have happened on any beach. Elaine, as a teenager, caught such a heavy fish she couldn't get it into the boat. She rowed ashore and dragged the fish up on the beach. This story turned up as fiction in one of Reed's novels, but could easily have started as fact.

Fishing particularly promotes story telling and we have been fishing those waters for possibly 100 years. There could be a volume filled with just fishing stories. Sadly we have neglected the tradition of sitting around the campfire repeating the family myths, generation after generation.

Cabin log entry, 1981. The beach absorbs children and provides limitless adventure and activity.

Chapter 7

DRIFT INN

"July 9, 1945: Back from three weeks on Whidbey. Completed revision of *Eagle's Wings*. Began outline for water front novel."[1]

—Reed Fulton

In 1943 Reed Fulton began a personal journal, which he kept daily until his death in 1957. He penned one brief entry each day. Sometimes the entries were as succinct as "Rain." Other times they included a sentence, rarely more. The cost of a new suit, his weight, the deer in his garden were subjects of note. Also, publication of his newest novel, speaking engagements, and trips to the cabin were recorded. I imagine Reed closing each day at his wooden roll-top desk in his second floor study with an entry into his journal. My guess is the journal resided in that roll-top desk since, with only one exception, Reed never recorded events on Whidbey.

Inez and Reed Fulton on the bluff at Ebey's Landing near Coupeville in 1946. On several occasions Reed and Inez used the Pratt home near here. When the social life at Clinton Beach became too busy and Reed was unable to concentrate on his writing, he and Inez escaped to this quiet haven.

An exception to the rule was one three-week stay on Whidbey in 1946 when he made daily entries; his longest entry being, "June 21, Cabin. Walked to point. Sunny, calm. Earthquake 9:30a.m. Dinner Oak Harbor. Mrs. Pratt in East." The reference to Oak Harbor, a town on the north end of Whidbey almost 40 miles from the cabin, and to Mrs. Pratt, a long-time friend and vacationer to the Coupeville area, located near Oak Harbor, leads me to conclude that this visit was to the Pratt house in Coupeville. I remember Inez explaining that the Clinton beach became very social with friends and relatives and Reed was unable to find the solitude to write. On at least one occasion they took the offer of Mrs. Pratt to visit her vacation cabin tucked privately in the woods on the bluff above Ebey's Landing on north Whidbey.

At some point before 1944, Inez and Reed stopped moving to camp for the summer. Elaine and Celeste were grown and married. By 1944 three grandchildren had joined the family. Sons-in-law Amos Wood and Jim Carpenter were away from home for long periods during World War II. During the summer of 1944 Reed worked for the war effort in Seattle, often at night. I suspect that Inez was busy assisting with us grandchildren. Inez and Reed never resumed their escape to the beach for more than a two- or three-week stay. They welcomed weekend retreats. The second World War signaled an end to the era of moving to the beach for the summer, at least for our family.

One surprising entry in Reed's journal on February 22, 1952 reads, "To Clinton, Kings offered $4,500 for camp." As a young child I don't remember a "For Sale" sign on the cabin, but I do remember talk of selling. Fifteen years earlier in 1927, Inez and Reed had purchased 11 acres and a small summer house on the west side of Mercer Island, in Lake Washington. By 1942 they had moved permanently from Seattle to that home and had substantially remodeled it. All three families, the Fultons, Woods, and Carpenters, lived on or had access to waterfront properties on Mercer Island. The young families were busy building homes and Inez and Reed extended their garden to include vegetables, fruit trees, and a formal rose garden, which required much of Reed's spare time. The beach cabin deteriorated with lack of care and use during the late 1940s and 1950s. This lack of use obviously initiated the talk of selling but, fortunately, it remained just talk. The cabin never sold and remained in the family, thank goodness!

We were not the only members of the greater Bakeman/Blackman clan to sag in our interest at the beach. Several cabins along the beach became rundown and seemingly forgotten during the 1940s and 1950s. Two of the three cabins owned by the original Blackman wives had already been sold out of the family. The third cabin would leave the family within the next generation.[2]

The cabin just to our south and originally bought by Elmer and Sylvia Lenfest passed to their one son, Norman. He never married and the cabin was sold after his death.[3]

Frances Bakeman Hodge and her brother, Ted, did retain their two cabins located on the original Bakeman 125 feet. Ted passed the old Bakeman cottage, (built, we think, by Reed Fulton) to his son Chuck, and constructed a newer connected cabin to the north for himself, his second wife Dorothy, and their expanding family.

"Beachcombing is not what you find, it is what you hope you will find."

— Amos Wood

We now pick up with my very earliest memories, around 1950, of going "down to camp." My father, Amos, was allocated only two weeks of vacation when I was growing up, so there was no luxury of spending a great deal of the summer at Whidbey. I remember we spent the long Fourth-of-July weekend and one or two weeks in August. We shared the cabin with our aunt Celeste Fulton Carpenter, her husband Jim, and our cousins Janet Sue, Sally, Bruce, and Steve. Occasionally Inez and Reed joined us, but that became more and more infrequent.

The events-of-the-summer when I was a child were the clamming and fishing parties attended by several close family friends from Mercer Island.[4] The families often hiked and camped together in the Cascades, so their gatherings at the beach were naturally called clam hikes. The farthest we hiked on these outings, however, was across the beach to row the dingy out to board the old 48-foot wooden yacht the *Regmar*. The most exciting destination was Hidden Island, an underwater shoal in Hood Canal, which became an island only on the lowest of low tides. The clams were abundant and we collected buckets full. On one adventure we filled the dingy, the *Clam Shell,* full of clams and towed it back to the cabin. The moms set up a work area on the back deck of the *Regmar* and used the return trip for a work party to shuck the clams. Big clams went through a grinder to be made into chowder.

A "clam hike" at Drift Inn in 1954. Several family friends from Mercer Island gathered at Clinton to dig clams, fish, and enjoy the beach. The Don Close, John Davis, David Davis, and Amos Wood families are pictured here.

Back at the cabin, we walked the beach looking for agates and beachcombing treasures. Family friend Dave Davis, clearly the champion agate finder, often sparked the interest of those with less keen eyes by salting the beach with some of his extras.

My father Amos was by far the most successful beachcomber— finding value in things many of us overlooked, such as one thong, pieces of rope, or a used plastic bottle. He justified such a find by explaining its use, "The mate to the thong would certainly be found the following day, the rope would be used to replace the bow rope on the *Clam Shell,* and the plastic bottle would make a dandy crab pot buoy float." We couldn't argue at the time, but after his death removed to the dump eight truckloads of old treasures still stashed in the boat house. He never found a glass ball at our Clinton beach, but definitely caught the beachcombing bug that led to his long-time avocation—writing about beachcombing, and especially the pursuit of Japanese glass fishing floats.[5]

Roasting dinner in a pit on the beach in 1951. Members of the Wood and Close families dig up potatoes which have been cooking with hot coals.

The extended family parties also included fishing. Boats of fishing hopefuls awoke at dawn, went out in the early morning, and successfully caught salmon and salmon trout enough for all. I can vividly recall awaking to the smell of fresh salmon trout being cooked for breakfast.

An afternoon activity for the children was fishing for sole. The preparation began with a jar and a stop behind the outhouse to find worms. My father made each of us three children our own hand-line fishing set-up. It consisted of a wooden board about the size and shape of a small cutting board. Each end had a large semi-circle removed to hold the line as it was wrapped around the board. Amos carved our initials in each one for identification and, he eternally hoped, avoidance of sibling squabbles. He then wrapped a dark green cotton line around and around the board and attached a sinker and a hook. Dad carefully demonstrated how to stick the hook into the wood for safety.

With our hand-line and a jar of worms we rowed out and tied to a buoy in about fifteen feet of water. A nice calm sunny afternoon was best. We wriggled a worm onto the hook (or asked our bigger, braver brother to do it), and dropped the hook and sinker over the side. We felt the line slacken when the weight hit bottom. Peering over the side into the calm water we could easily observe any interest in our bait, a pale irregular blob against the sandy bottom. The flat-bodied sole and flounder tentatively dislodged from their camouflaged position half-buried in the sand and first inspected, then bit at our bait. We caught a dozen in an afternoon. To keep the numbers of sole in check Mom announced, "You have to clean what you catch." Cleaning the sole took much longer than catching them.

Amos Wood with two good-looking fish.

Another tradition at the cabin was the Fourth of July celebration.[6] Weeks prior to the three-day vacation, Amos and my brother Dick ordered, from Ace Fireworks somewhere-back-east, a whole box full of non-safe and non-sane fireworks. Fancy sky rockets, 2" Salutes, cherry bombs, buzz bombs, lady fingers—things that were not available to purchase at local shops—arrived by railroad express. (The fireworks I enjoyed were the snakes that burned an ash on the sidewalk and didn't make a noise at all.) The neighbors joined us on the porch curled up in blankets to "Ohhh" and "Ahhh" at the spectacle. Dick has religiously kept this tradition alive with the help of fireworks purchased at the Tulalip Indian Reservation across the bay.

Vacationing at the cabin meant that the sandy, endless beach was our playground. The extremes of tides provided variety and change, from finding fool's gold at the waters edge at minus tides, to fishing off the bulkhead at high tide. Our games evolved from the structure of the beach. A walk to the Sawdust Dock included the challenge of walking the whole distance on beach logs. We even carried a small flat stick to fling out and use as a stepping stone if the logs became too far apart. We looked for a solid sandy beach to draw the large circle and cross paths required for "Fox and Geese." When the sun set and the tide came in the games moved ashore with "Kick the Can" as we ran around and hid among the cabins and dinghies pulled up above high tide.

Getting a fish-cleaning lesson from Don Close in 1949. The rule was: if you caught 'um, you had to clean 'um. But then you also got to eat 'um.

I'm in the center, paying close attention to the lesson but, sadly, with no fish to practice on.

There were two rules for us kids at the beach: don't climb the cliff without an adult nearby, and keep your legs on the grass side when sitting on the bulkhead. The first rule made sense to me having seen the results of the cliffs sliding. Prior to the second rule on an unrecorded summer day sometime around 1952, my younger sister Nancy was sitting on the seven-foot high bulkhead. Her feet were dangling on the water side with the tide out. About four years old at the time, she was seated right next to Mom. Somehow, over she went with a thud. Lots of commotion and the diagnosis of a broken collarbone solidified that rule.

All the boats had names in 1956. Dick Wood is in the Clam Shell, *a boat he helped construct. In the* Drift Wood, *from left to right, are Frances Wood, Charlotte Mowrer, Nancy Wood, and Elaine Wood.*

Back then all the boats had names. Even the dingy wasn't called just "the dingy;" it had a name and the name was painted on the stern. For years our dingy was the *Clam Shell*, constructed by Amos and Dick as a father-son project one winter in Amos's workshop. I remember it as the winter we smelled fiberglass fumes escaping from the workshop into the house. Subsequent dinghies have been called the *Clam Chowder* and the *Clam Dip*. Maybe you catch the theme. The dinghies were used, and still are, to row from shore to crab pots or to larger boats moored to buoys. For many years our fishing boat was a flat-bottomed, wide, heavy, wooden boat called the *Drift Wood*. A seven-horsepower Evinrude outboard motor propelled the heavy boat through the water, at just about trolling speed.

During the 1950s, under the supervision of Amos, changes began appearing at the cabin. First, it was given a name, the Drift Inn. The original name, Camp Illahee, was never used by my family, and after a generation of the cabin's being nameless, Amos selected an old oar, painted the name and installed it. I don't remember any discussion or a name-the-cabin contest, it just happened. Giving the cabin a new name may have been only symbolic, but it initiated the momentum for a series of changes that began to revive our tired old cabin back into life.

A giant step forward was the installation of a real flush toilet and indoor bathroom. Later the kitchen, which was located on the enclosed back porch, was moved to the front facing the bay. Water for washing and the toilet was supplied to the cabin from a stream flowing off the bank. About half-way up the hill, a series of barrels collected the water and allowed the sand and silt to settle before entering pipes that flowed down to the house. Our neighbor, Norman Lenfest, had a wonderfully clear well, and we used a bucket to haul this fresh water to our house for drinking.

Probably the steepest road that many of us have ever driven now provides vehicular access through a deep, wooded ravine at the north end of Clinton Beach. That road was constructed during the 1950s by Bob Hastings to develop and sell beach lots on property he owned north of the ravine. In August of 1978, the Hastings Road Beach Club was founded to manage and maintain the road easements and the parking stalls for its twenty members. Now, instead of walking from the south past nineteen cabins to reach our house, we walk from the north in front of ten cabins.

During the late 1960s the piling bulkhead, which had been installed by Inez and Reed shortly after the purchase of the cabin in 1930, was badly deteriorating to an extent that some of our yard had eroded away, particularly the land to the northern end of our lot. In 1972, my grandmother, Inez, hired Mr. Scrivens for a price of $6,869 to build a new concrete bulkhead and boat ramp.

The summer of 1967 was a busy one for Amos and Elaine with the marriages of their two oldest offspring, and it was also the year of the publication of Amos's book, *Beachcombing for Japanese Glass Floats*. Unlike Reed, who did much of his research and writing at the cabin, Amos researched and wrote at his home on Mercer Island. However, the techniques of beachcombing explained in his books were born on our many hikes around the shores of Whidbey Island. Later the rewards of beachcombing the Pacific beaches lured Amos to the outer beaches of Washington, Oregon, and British Columbia. These became Amos's favorite beachcombing haunts, but he never passed up a chance to check out what might have washed up with the last tide on the long undeveloped beach north of the cabin.

Nancy and Dick Wood with their proud catch in 1954.

After Reed's death in 1957, Inez retained ownership of the cabin with most of the maintenance and use taken over by Elaine and Amos and their three children.

Years later, Nancy Wood Oyler with crew in the Clam Chowder.

> Dec 28, 1995.
> Francie, Munro and Catherine came up to the beach cabin for a day. Munro's first time in three years, Catherine's first time ever. We're going back to NYC next week but are glad to see the mountains and walk the beaches before heading back to the city.

Cabin log entry, 1995. Now Dick, Nancy, and myself share the cabin with the next generation. We hope the feeling of going "down to camp" will be carried forward.

Chapter 8

PRESENT GENERATION

This book began with noting the first entry in the cabin Log by Grandmother B (Nina) in 1937. For the next 30 years there were odds and ends of entries and gaps of decades. Finally in about 1967, we got into the habit of writing in the log at the end of each visit. With such on-the-spot recording of history, there is little need to duplicate it here; however, I have included some tasty tidbits from the cabin log.

There are a few highlights that deserve more than a brief report in the log. An example is the history behind the diving platform constructed on the piling in front of the cabin to the south. The lone piling probably stood there 100 feet off shore for 30 years, collecting barnacles and holding up gulls until one summer my then college-age sister, Nancy, and our cousin Bruce Carpenter, had a vision. It was the perfect diving/jumping platform minus some steps up and a platform on top. Days of construction in the boathouse and installation from a tied-up dinghy followed. We eagerly awaited the perfect high tide for christening. It was Bruce who first crawled up the eight cross-bars and stood poised like an Olympic diver on the platform. He bowed to the crowd assembled on shore, bowed several more times, looked over the side, and called down to Nancy hovering in a dinghy near by. We missed his words, but did hear her shouted response, "Then I'll go!" That was enough to push his psyche forward. He squeezed his nose with thumb and finger and jumped in, looking like he was sitting in a chair. We cheered the attempt, gave him a "2" for style, and the piling has never been the same.

The year 1972 signaled a turning of the tide for our cabin. That was the year the new bulkhead was built, which spurred the impetus for badly needed upkeep on the cabin. I remember Dick and I felt we could easily lose one of our cherished new offspring, not by falling into the bay, but by falling through the floorboards in the deteriorating hallway to the back door.

Interest in using the cabin had returned, Inez was willing with the purse, strong young labor was ready and willing, so we began a decade of cabin renewal. Inez was very willing to pay for repairs with one restriction, "Do what you want but always keep the lines of the cabin." She was referring to the original

Drift Inn getting a new porch roof in about 1976. Elaine Wood on scaffolding.

lines that J. S. White had carefully designed into the cabin in the 1910s. We started at the bottom with new cement pillar foundations and a re-leveling of the main cabin during 1972-3. A new porch was built in 1973 and a new kitchen the next year; 1976 brought new wiring in the big cabin and a new porch roof. In 1983 we agreed to hire local builder, Dick Day, to remodel the interior. The whole back section of the cabin was rebuilt with a new bathroom, complete with hot water and shower, three storage closets (one for each of the three families), and a downstairs bedroom to replace the old bathroom. The north wall of the living room was pushed out to enclose the old sleeping porch. The old fireplace and chimney were removed and a wood stove and stovepipe installed. Whew! All this and we kept the lines.

By 1980, the Little House was raised to allow room for a boathouse and storage area underneath. Amos engineered and completed that house-raising.

The late 1970s brought water system woes. We struggled with the barrel system then attempted to dig a well. These problems continued into the mid-1980s until city water arrived and our generations-old headache vanished. The fallout from that solution is that now we have so much water we are plagued by septic tank backup.

All of that work deserved a party, so in July of 1986 we celebrated with a cabin reunion. We invited the relatives and friends who had regularly visited the beach through the generations. Over fifty came. The beach Olympics were held with clamshell medals. We beachcombed, played "Fox and Geese," spit watermelon seeds off the bulkhead, jumped off the piling and, you guessed it, ate clam chowder. It felt good to again do all the familiar family traditions. Deep in my bones, it felt really, really good.

One benefit of getting all the major cabin remodel behind us is that we now have time for other pleasures and creativity. If we are to judge by what has been recorded recently in the log, much of that pleasure and creativity has evolved around cooking. Dick and Cathy have definitely pushed our culinary expectations to a new high, aided, undoubtedly, by the installation of a newer stove and oven. The abundance of fresh seafood—especially crab, clams, and mussels—has undoubtedly inspired their seafood recipe repertoire. Their recipes have won highest awards in local and national cooking competitions. Here is their award-winning recipe for Clinton Beach Clam Chowder.

Elaine and Amos Wood in 1978, in front of the Little House (where Reed did his writing). It has been raised to accomodate a shop area underneath and guests above.

Clinton Beach Clam Chowder

8 ounces bacon, cut in small pieces
2 ribs celery
1/2 pound mushrooms, sliced
1 bunch green onion, cut in rounds
6 pounds "steamer" clams
2 cups half-and-half
1 tablespoon cumin
2 tablespoons flour
Salt and pepper
2 tablespoons cilantro, minced

Cook bacon in frying pan until golden brown; remove half of the bacon and drain on paper towels. Add celery, green onions, potatoes, and mushrooms to remaining bacon and sauté about 5 minutes. Scrub clam shells. Steam the clams in a splash of water or white wine until they are just open. Remove clams from shells. Add clam broth to bacon/vegetable mixture and cook until potatoes are tender, about 15 minutes. Add half-and-half and heat 2 minutes, making sure chowder doesn't boil. Add cumin, heat, and thicken with flour, about 5 minutes. Add clams at the last minute to heat through. Salt and pepper to taste. Ladle into bowls, garnish with cilantro and remaining bacon. Makes six servings, preparation time about 40 minutes. Enjoy!

Dick and Cathy's creativity often happens in the kitchen. Here is one of many seafood-inspired recipes in their repertoire.

Inez continued to visit and enjoy the cabin almost until her death in 1977 at the age of 89. With her passing the ownership transferred to her oldest daughter, Elaine. Inez's second daughter, Celeste, had preceded her mother in death. Elaine owned the cabin for four years before she died in 1981, when Dick, Nancy, and I inherited Drift Inn. It has been enjoyed by our three families in common ever since, with little rancor except with regard to Dick's flair for decorating.

Nancy Wood Oyler's birhtday, May 14, 1978. Interior of cabin shows firplace and mantel made from bircks processed at the old Brickyard on the beach.

Left to right: Lee Wood, Nancy, husband Duane Oyler, Mark Wood, and Dick Wood. Head of Matthew or Nathanael Wood in foreground.

Two of Aunt Celeste's children, Janet Sue and Sally, purchased land and subsequently built a beach house on Hartstene Island in southern Puget Sound, closer to their homes in the Auburn area. We hope their new camp will become infused with all the traditions and joys we have experienced together as cousins at Drift Inn. The concept of going "down to camp" is ultimately transferable. Our particular speck of land on Whidbey has no corner on the market for summer folk experiencing renewal, refreshment, adventure, and creativity.

The key is to take the time, slow down, let your rhythm seek a balance with nature. We need to take long, mindless beach walks. A very important element of going "down to camp" is to leave our city toys in the city. They confuse and complicate our lives. And worse, they distract us from hearing the waves, seeing the endlessly variable cloud formations, smelling the fresh salty air, and finding out what is really going on deep down in our core. If we transfer our rushed, harried, electronically stimulated city life to the country, it succeeds only in turning the country into the city. Then there is no sanctuary, there is no retreat, there is no creativity. We are still separated from the natural healing effects of rubbing next to nature. There will be no reason to build a sand castle.

Cabin reunion in 1986. After almost a decade of cabin renovation we celebrated with a reunion, inviting the family and friends who have been regular visitors at the cabin.

The rest of the history is all in the cabin log: exploding fruit on the Fourth of July; fishing trips to Baby Island; grandparents visiting from Walla Walla; American flags sticking out of red geranium pots; friends who joined us for the weekend; pink flamingos; name and phone number of the guy who will mow the lawn; the description of trying to convince a hermit crab that he needs a newer shell, and much, much more.

Today the cabin is no longer neglected but instead is in great demand during the summer months. The three families are invited to the three long holiday weekends of the summer. I invite my women's group to celebrate the summer solstice each year. Nancy brings her soccer team to a retreat. Dick has a "rendezvous" with friends at the close of the summer season, very loosely following the native American tradition of the potlatch. Between those events the weekends are taken by our generation and, now, the next generation.

We don't go "down to camp" by boat any more, we don't visit Camp Illahee or get our milk at the Old Clinton dock store. Most of the year we can't even fish, with the depleted salmon runs and restrictions to protect the few remaining fish. But "camp" really hasn't changed. The clams are still there in abundance, crab still get lured into the trap by a can of cat food, the beach needs to be combed, and agates remain to be found. The gulls still drop clams on the roof of the cabin. The great blue heron still squawks four times in a row, and the ramshackle old cabin still sits on the most spectacular beach in all of Puget Sound.

One of the Olympic-type events at the reunion was the tideflat race. The winners were not the hefty strong teenaged boys but the lithe skinny little girls.

Cabin log entry, 1996. Today the expanding families enjoy the cabin in many different ways. But the reasons we retreat are the same as in the 1900s.

Chapter 9

CONCLUSION

Why do we keep coming back year after year and generation after generation? Why have you, my sons, made me promise, with my most sacred pledge, that I will never sell the cabin or give up my one-third share? It is partly that it represents our roots, a continuous family connection for almost 100 years. It is the place I think of when I think of going home. It is a place I can easily visualize my parents, particularly my mother, smiling. It holds the history and heritage of who we are.

Partly, it is unique since it hasn't changed much in those 100 years. Neither growing industry nor increased land value has pushed us out. The few businesses that were active on the beach have left, gone out of business, gone out of purpose. The unstable hill and walk-in aspects have kept big fancy expensive homes from overwhelming our cabin flavor. It is so much the same as when Nina and Charles first came here that they would recognize it at a glance.

Cousins born ten days apart, Munro Galloway (left) and Mark Wood hanging out together. They have a long, squishy walk to the water at low tide.

Also, another part of the answer is that it truly is an exquisitely beautiful and scenic place. The panorama of mountains starts with Mt. Baker and Shuksan. Then Whitehorse, Pilchuck, Index and, if you go out in a boat or up to the top of the hill, even the master of the range, Mt. Rainier, can be seen. Two islands break up the mainland behind and provide destinations for boating. Even Everett, with its ecological problems, looks innocent and clean as it sparkles at us once the sun sets. And there is the water: the bay, the wulge, Possession Sound, with all its infinite shades of colors, textures, winds, waves, and tides. It allows us to experience the simple magic of nature.

Going "down to camp" is many things. It is watching as the crab pot just breaks the surface with expectation of crab for dinner. It is feeling around for butter clams in the cool murky clamming hole. Scoping a flock of Caspian Tern feeding in one giant oval between the old Shell Dock and the Sawdust Dock. Hearing the ratchety call of the kingfisher. Awakening with the klunk of a clam hitting the roof, dropped by a gull looking for a hard surface to crack the shell. And the special times for the patient and lucky: seeing a pod of Orca, which, for some unexplained reason, choose our passage rather than Admiralty Inlet. Observing a gray whale lazily feeding right in front of the cabin.

Quietly eyeing an innocently unafraid baby seal parked on the sand to rest while its mother is off feeding. Enjoying porpoise dancing with the bow wake of the ferry, when our car is parked right at the bow. All of these events I have personally experienced at the beach, and wish each of you the same and more. One thing I will guarantee is that you won't experience them unless you spend time there.

If I had to come up with one answer, the real answer as to why we come to the cabin, I truly believe the answer is time. The cabin allows us the luxury of leisure time. Free time is now a scarce commodity becoming seriously endangered. Where else can you justify spending two hours looking for agates? Or five hours sitting in a boat with a pole and line? Here we are physically separated from our daily to-do list. The demands of home can wait, the energy to keep the cabin going is minimal. At the cabin it is OK to putter—to paint clam shells bright colors, to make a sand castle, to collect sea glass, to bake things from scratch. We play gin rummy or hearts, something we never do in town.

One of the strongest memories I have of a specific day at the beach is not a day writing or beachcombing or birding or boating or fishing or picking blackberries. We have done those many times on many days. But I do remember a day that I sat in the hammock and watched the tide go out and watched the tide come back in again. Yes, it takes over eight hours for that much tide change. And no, I wasn't sick. I did do some reading, napping, and kept my binoculars handy. But mainly it was a day with absolutely no agenda. It was a day that refreshed me to the depths of my soul. I consider it a day well spent.

Where, but at the cabin, could I have found the time.

FOOTNOTES

Chapter 2

[1] South Whidbey Historical Society, *South Whidbey and Its People, Vol. 1*, 1983, page 81.
[2] South Whidbey Historical Society, *South Whidbey and Its People, Vol. 1*, 1983, page 131.
[3] Elizabeth Dodge, *Island County: A World Beater*, 1910, page 14.

Chapter 3

[1] Remembrances of George Clark IV, grandson of Inza and George Clark, Mission Viejo, CA, August 1992. Some of his information was not first-hand, but came to him from his grandparents and aunts.
[2] *The Snohomish Story 1859-1959*, "My Father, Charlie Bakeman," by Frances Bakeman Hodge, page 20.
[3] Letter from Arthur Blackman to Nina Blackman, his sister.
[4] Family history letter to John and Paul Hodge written by their mother, Frances Bakeman Hodge.
[5] Unfinished novel by Frances Bakeman Hodge.
[6] Family history letter to John and Paul Hodge written by their mother, Frances Bakeman Hodge.

Chapter 4

[1] Family history letter to John and Paul Hodge written by their mother, Frances Bakeman Hodge
[2] There is no record of a fourth Blackman brother, William, who settled in Seattle, owning property on Clinton Beach. However, the casual clannish camping could have allowed sharing of areas without purchasing the land. William was married to Ada Foss, a common New England name.

[3] Mary married Eugene Lenfest in Bradley, Maine before moving to Snohomish in 1889. Their one son, Elmer, was born while the family was still in Maine in 1864. By the year 1903, when her younger brothers' wives were purchasing property at Clinton, Mary was near sixty. Her son Elmer, however, was at a logical age to be looking for summer property. A successful civil engineer, he was elected as Snohomish County surveyor. Elmer married Sylvia M. Ferguson, the daughter of E. C. Ferguson, the founding pioneer of Snohomish. Their one child, Norman, was born in 1893.

[4] Continuing south from the Blackman land came the Knapp clan, one of whom, Ella, had already intermarried with the Blackman clan. Ella's brother, Cyrus Knapp, married a Burke daughter. The original Burke family had three daughters, so the surname was lost, but several cabins are still owned by Burke progeny. Next came the Clark family who owned, and still own, cabins between the Burke property and the end of the Brighton Beach Road. The Clarks were not original beach people, but early on George Clark married Inza Knapp. Inza brought George to the beach and he brought his two brothers, Lew and Click, and a sister, Hazel Clark Blair. So all three original beach families, the Blackmans, Knapps, and Burkes, and later the Clarks, are related by marriage.

[5] Remembrances of George Clark IV, Mission Viejo, CA, August 1992.

[6] Recorded interview with Margaret Amelia Clark Mykut, by Charles and Joan Bakeman, at the Bakeman Cottage, Clinton Beach, August 6, 1995.

[7] South Whidbey Historical Society, *South Whidbey and Its People*, Vol. I, 1983, page 133.

[8] The dance hall was located between the present Rogers property and the Sladky/Day property.

[9] The original gable-roofed cabin is in the position of the present Samuelson's property. An unsigned, undated note on the back of the photo referring to the gabled house in the center of the photo says, "The original Bakeman house at Clinton Beach—at location of Frances and Paul's [Hodge] house now. Sleeping tent to the north is at current location of C. 'Ted' Bakeman." It is unclear if this original house was built when Nina and Charles purchased the property or built soon thereafter. The absence of a newer cabin built in 1913 dates this picture prior to that date.

[10] There is a hand-written, undated, unrecorded (and therefore not legal) "quit claim deed" from Nina and Charles to Inez and Reed for 56 feet, which about matches the position of that cabin. We assume something sufficed to transferred ownership to Reed and Inez since later in 1930 they legally sold the cabin to Ted.

[11] Recorded conversation with Harriet Putnam at Lagoon Point, July 1996. Harriet and her two sisters Helen and Margery were Reed's nieces and came to camp for visits with their cousins Elaine and Celeste Fulton.

[12] Interview with George Clark IV, July 1995.

[13] Written remembrances of Clinton Beach by Charles D. Bakeman, November 1996.

[14] Written remembrances of Clinton Beach by Charles D. Bakeman, November 1996.

Chapter 5

[1] *Illahee Magazine,* Kirkland, WA

[2] Letter from Mrs. D. M. Taylor (Nettie Morgan) to Inez Fulton dated Feb. 17, 1930.

[3] Letter from Mrs. D. M. Taylor (Nettie Morgan) to Inez Fulton dated Jan. 26, 1930.

[4] Letter from Mrs. D. M. Taylor (Nettie Morgan) to Inez Fulton dated Jan. 26, 1930.

[5] Letter from Mrs. D. M. Taylor (Nettie Morgan) to Inez Fulton dated March 3, 1930.

[6] Letter from Mrs. D. M. Taylor (Nettie Morgan) to Inez Fulton dated Feb. 17, 1930.

[7] Reprinted in *The Snohomish Story* by the Snohomish Centennial Association in 1959.

[8] Letter from Mrs. D. M. Taylor (Nettie Morgan) to Inez Fulton dated Feb. 17, 1930.

[9] Letter from Elmer Lenfest of Snohomish to H. Reed Fulton of Seattle, Feb. 9, 1931.

[10] Recorded conversation with Charles D. Bakeman, Sept., 1996

[11] Recorded conversation with Charles D. Bakeman, Sept., 1996

[12] A slide destroyed another cabin years ago that was located between the present Touhy house and the Larson-Brown house. Walking by, you can't help but notice the large side gardens between those houses. After the house in between was destroyed by slide, the owners on each side bought half of the now cabinless lot and incorporated the land into garden and boat house.

Chapter 6

[1] South Whidbey Historical Society, *South Whidbey and Its People, Volume II,* 1985, page 62.

[2] Chinook jargon meaning deep waters.

[3] Story recounted by Ted's son Jeff Bakeman, August 1996.

Chapter 7

[1] Personal Journal of Reed Fulton 1943-1957.

[2] Alanson and Eliza Blackman had no children and early-on their camp was purchased by the George Clark family and later sold to the Schaffer family. Elhanon and Frances Blackman had one daughter, Edith Blackman Morris, who owned the cabin before it was sold to the Evans family. (Edith also purchased a cabin, later called "Camp Lew," and presently owned by Robert and Ione Blair.) Hyrcanus and Ella passed their camp to their daughter Eunice, who married Dr. William Ford. (Hyrcanus and Ella's son, Clifford Blackman, married Maude Morgan, so they had use of Camp Illahee until Clifford died in 1920 and the Morgans sold in 1930.) Eunice and William Ford passed their cabin to their one daughter, Phyllis, who married George Bican. Finally, the original Ella and Hyrcanus Blackman camp was sold to Dick and Judy Day.

[3] Wally and Becky Erickson purchased the Lenfest cabin and later sold to the present owners, the Rogers.

[4] The David T. Davis family, with Jean, JoAnn, and Robin, and the Close family (Don, Ruth Mary, Dick, Marilyn, Cathy, David, Frank and later Christie) were the most frequent visitors. That group often expanded to include the John Davis family, with Ruth, Jean, Mac, Bruce, Ann, Margaret, and Elizabeth. On occasion, the Lucas's and the Spikards joined as well.

[5] Amos' books included: *Beachcombing for Japanese Glass Floats, Beachcombing the Pacific,* and *Hiking Trails in the Pacific Northwest.*

[6] Dave and Charlotte Mowrer with their children, Bruce and Elaine (named for my mother), joined us for many years.

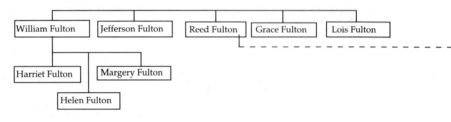

FAMILY TREE

BLACKMAN FAMILY

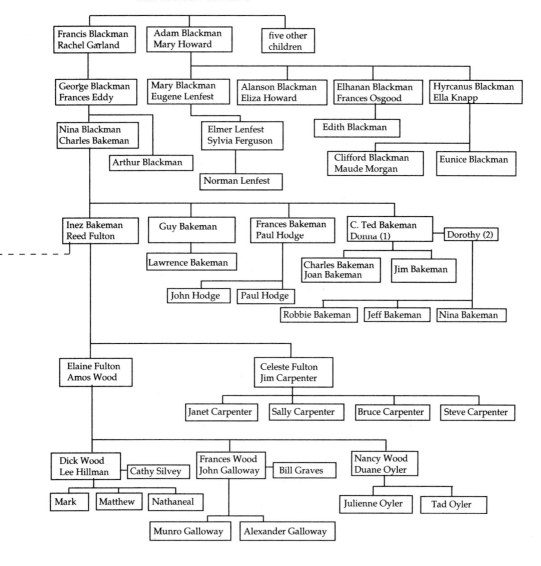

113

HISTORY OF CABIN OWNERSHIP

Camps between Hastings Road and the garages on Brighton Beach Road (north to south). Prior owners in parentheses; present owners in all caps.

    HEBNER, Phil B. and Addi

    (Hebner, Phil and Lucy)
    DIMM, Chris Hebner & Don

    (Chambers, Bryce and Helen Hastings)
    (Chambers, Collin)
    BUTLER, Bill & Liz

    CHILDS, Art and Doris [Art's mother was
        Bob Hastings' sister]

    (Brennan, George)
    (Kruze, Henry)
    (Sigurdson/Bjorn)
    LARSON-BROWN, Eric

    (Durrant, Dudley)
    (Stevens, Roy, and Adam)
    Property divided between Brennan and
        Hansen following a slide.

    (Turner, Gilbert "Gib")
    (Hansen, Pete)
    (Hansen, Thor "Tov")
    TOUHY, Tom and Judy

(Bailey, Earl)
(Mero, Eddie [B's ? older brother])
(Mero, Billy, and Mabel)
(Touhy, Cedric and Beatrice Mero)
TOUHY, Ced and Ann
MORGAN, Harvery and Claire Touhy
TOUHY, Craig and Marilyn

1902 (Snyder, and Dr. McCready)
1912 (Bakeman, Charles Henry and Nina Blackman)
1913@ (Fulton, Reed and Inez Bakeman)
1930 (Bakeman, Charles "Ted" and Dorothy)
BAKEMAN, Jeff and Mary, Nina and Robbie
BAKEMAN, Chuck and Joan, Kathy Bakeman
Bernhoft "Bakeman Cottage"

1912 (Bakeman, Charles Henry and Nina Blackman)
(Hodge, Paul and Frances Bakeman)
"Hodge Podge Lodge"
(Wallace, Dee)
SAMUELSON, Steve and Lori (Slide demolished home in March of 1990)

1902 (Morgan, Alonza and Agnus)
(Wolcott, Bill)
(Chase, Bill and Phylis Wolcot)
1996 COX, Greg and Annette

1902 (Morgan, Ben Sr. and Nettie) "Illahee"
1930 (Fulton, Reed and Inez Bakeman)
1977 (Wood, Amos and Elaine Fulton) "Drift Inn"
1981 WOOD, Richard and Cathy Silvey
WOOD, Frances and William Graves
OYLER, Nancy Wood and Duane

1902   (Lenfest, Elmer and Sylvia) Elmer was son of
             Mary Blackman and Eugene Lenfest
        (Lenfest, Norman)
        (Erickson, Wally and Becky)
        ROGERS, Bob and Gloria

Empty lot with old dance pavilion and community dock

1903   (Blackman, Hyrcanus and Ella Knapp)
        (Ford, Eunice Blackman [daughter of Hyrcanus
             and Ella Blackman])
        (Bican, Phyllis Ford)
        (Day, Dick and Judy)
        SLADKY, Eric and Judy Day

1906   (Blackman, Elhanan and Frances Osgood)
        (Morris, W.C. and Edith Blackman [daughter of
             Elhanan])
        (Evans, Charles and Frank and Mcro, Eddie)
        (Evans, Margaret [sister of Charles])
        BRADSMA, Cor and Ester Vik

        (Clark, Lew)
        (Chappell, Albert)
        BEALS, Ralph and Cora

        (Crane, Pat)
        (Crane, Walt)
        (Olson)
        (Carpenter, Lyle and Nina Austin)
        RICE, Keith and Roberta

1903   (Blackman, Alanson and Eliza)
        (Clark, George II and Inza Knapp) "Pioneer"
        (Schaffer, Phil and Alice)
        SCHAFFER, Jim and Phil, Jr.

Originally two camps—"HooRah's Nest" and "Shark's Tooth Shoal"

        (Knapp, Cyrus and Amelia Burke)
        (Clark, Inza Knapp [niece of Amelia Burke])
        (Brown)
        SPANGLER, Jerry and Margaret Eckstrom
                "HooRah's Nest"

        (Knapp, Cyrus and Amelia Burke) "Camp Kozy"
        (Clark, Inza Knapp [niece of Amelia Burke])
        (Kimball)
        KNAPP, Steve and Elaine—no relation to original
                Knapp family

        (Cudney, Roy and Mary Pilz)
        (Hunt, Howard and Ada Cudney) "Dun Work Inn"
        SCHWENN, Steve and Kathy

        (Hoag)
        STEVENSON, Dugan and Vicky Van Diest

        (Kinney)
        (Olson)
        (Stiger, Tom)
        (Eckstrom, Andy and Tom)
        ECKSTROM, Tom Jr. and Joann
        HONG, Suzanne Eckstrom

(Inkster, Rusty and Alice) "Temple of Purity"
(Fosness, Ken and Sue Clark [daughter of
 Click Clark])
ENGSTROM, Kevin and Jill

(Stafford)
(Clark, Earl "Click" and Beulah)
(Mackie, Nathalia "Tally" Clark [daughter of
 Click Clark])
HAGLAND, Victor

(Bell, Walter and Lilian Blackman [daughter of
 Almon* Blackman])
 *Almon was first cousin of Hyrcanus,
 Alanson, and Elhanon Blackman

(Clark, George I and Katherine)
(Clark, Lew) "Camp Lew"
BLAIR, Robert and Ione

(Boyd)
(Cleveland, Howard and Susie)
GREEN, Les and Ellen Jane "E.J." Cleveland

(Headly)
(Carpenter, Lyle and Nina)
(Jones, Edward and Lucille)
BLAIR, L. V. "Pete" and Lynn

(Kingsby, Grace F.)
1936 (Fulton, Lois and Grace [sisters of Reed Fulton])
(Fulton, Jefferson [Reed's nephew])
HISKEN, Pete and Marionette

(Blair, Vern and Hazel Clark [sister of Lew and Click Clark])
BLAIR, Lorraine and Bud (deceased) "Blair House"

(Johnson, Ellen Burke [aunt to Margaret Mykut])
(Knapp, Inza and George Clark II)
MYKUT, Margaret Clark [daughter of Inza Knapp and George Clark II]

BRADFORD (trailer)

(Bridgford, Alice Burke [aunt of Margaret Mykut])
(Knapp, Dr. Cullen [uncle of Margaret Mykut])
(West, John W. and Elsie Winston)
WEST, John "Jack" Jr. and Myrna Vail

SALISBURY, Clark and Isabelle

KNAPP, Art and Inez
KNAPP, Dick and Jean

ECKSTROMS

PETERSEN, Billy and Bea

SALISBURY, Dallas

ECKSTROM, Tommy (in cabin)

Lots owned by SAMPSON

THORESON, Wendell (deceased) and Beth Galbreath

WRIGHTSMAN, [grandson of H. Hinman)

THE GARAGES